T0265615

The Modern and Perfecting Rite of Symbolic Masonry

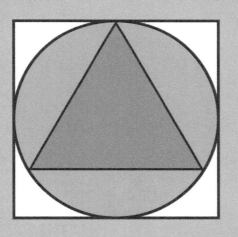

A Freemasonic Reformation
To the Glory of the Enlightened Humanity
and
A Movement for a
Humanistic World Order

Nicolas Laos

Published by:
Trine Day LLC
PO Box 577
Walterville, OR 97489
1-800-556-2012
www.TrineDay.com
trineday@icloud.com

Library of Congress Control Number: 2022948759

Laos, Nicolas,
The Modern And Perfecting Rite Of Symbolic Masonr—1st ed.
p. cm.
Epub (ISBN-13) 978-1-63424-421-3
Trade Paper (ISBN-13) 978-1-63424-420-6
Cloth (ISBN-13) 978-1-63424-419-0
1. Freemasonry—History. 2. Freemasonry—Religious Aspects. 3. Freemason-
ry—Political Aspercts. 4. Freemasonry—New I. Title

FIRST EDITION
10 9 8 7 6 5 4 3 2 1

Printed in the USA
Distribution to the Trade by:
Independent Publishers Group (IPG)
814 North Franklin Street
Chicago, Illinois 60610
312.337.0747
www.ipgbook.com

ACQUIRE THE REAL

GNOSIS

CONTENTS

Preface 1

Frequent Abbreviations 7

Chapter 1: Fundamental Concepts 9

Chapter 2: Initiatory Systems 33

Chapter 3: The Modern and Perfecting Rite of Symbolic Masonry 71

THIS BOOK IS A FREEMASONIC MANIFESTO, A REFERENCE WORK, AND AN ESOTERIC COMPENDIUM

I was born on 2 July 1974, in Athens, Greece. I was initiated into Freemasonry in 1997 in London, England ("Honor Per Onus Lodge," No. 6586, United Grand Lodge of England, under Grand Master Prince Edward, Duke of Kent; I was raised to the degree of a Master Mason in the same Lodge). I was awarded the 33rd degree of the Ancient and Accepted Scottish Rite and a relevant Patent in 2017, in Rome, Italy (Ordine Massonico Tradizionale Italiano-Supremo Consiglio del Rito Scozzese Antico e Accettato Tradizionale d'Italia, under Grand Master Luigi Pruneti), and I became officially affiliated with the Supreme Council of the Traditional Ancient and Accepted Scottish Rite of Italy in 2020 (under Sovereign Grand Commander Br. Giovanni Constantini). I was awarded the

95th degree of the Ancient and Primitive Rite of Memphis–Misraim and a relevant Patent in 2012, in Atlanta, Georgia, U.S.A. (Lodge of the "Sons and Daughters of Aaron" under Grand Hierophant Tau Allen H. Greenfield, Bertiaux lineage), I was awarded the 97th degree and a relevant Patent in 2015, in Vršak, Serbia ("Misir" Lodge under Grand Hierophant Tau Neven Daničić, Bertiaux lineage), and, as a Grand Hierophant 97°, I joined the Sovereign Italian Sanctuary of the Egyptian Rite of Misraim (Sovrano Santuario Italiano del Rito Egizio di Misraïm) in 2020.

Furthermore, I wish to acknowledge the role that Professor Giuliano Di Bernardo has played in my esoteric education. He is an internationally renowned philosopher and Freemason. In 1979, Dr. Giuliano di Bernardo was awarded a full professorship in Philosophy of Science and Logic at the Faculty of Sociology of the University of Trento, where he occupied the chair until 2010. He was installed as the Grand Master of the Grand Orient of Italy (Grande Oriente d'Italia) in 1990. After three years, he resigned and founded the Regular Grand Lodge of Italy (Gran Loggia Regolare d'Italia), which was immediately recognized by English Freemasonry. In 2002, having decided that he had completed his work in conventional, regular Freemasonry, he founded the Order of the Illuminati (Ordine degli Illuminati), not as a passive and atavistic imitation of Adam Weishaupt's Bavarian Illuminati, but as an updated and philosophically informed initiatory society of "the Invisibles who plan the material and moral development of humanity." Grand Master Dr. Giuliano Di Bernardo, in his capacity as the head of the Academy of the Illuminati (Accademia degli Illuminati), based in Rome at Piazza di Spagna, has officially conferred upon me the power and the principles of the Illuminati, and he has officially conferred upon me the power and the privileges to form in Greece the National Headquarters of the Illuminati.

I have created a new Masonic Rite, and I have called it the "Modern and Perfecting Rite of Symbolic Masonry" (in my mother Greek language: "Νεωτερικός και Τελεσιουργικός Τύπος του Συμβολικού Τεκτονισμού").

In the Spring of 2008, a small group of Freemasons and other distinguished men and women of the civil society, who were provisionally styled as the "Scholarly and Political Order of the Ur-Illuminati," or a "Masonic Society of Illuminists," met at an office in Wilton Road, in South West London, accepted me as its chairman, and we decided to undertake and accomplish a difficult and bold Project regarding the reformation of Freemasonry along the lines that I explain in this book. Gradually, many Freemasonic, scientific, and philosophical adepts as well as business people and technocrats from around the world embarked on this Project. During 2008-21, several well-protected meetings took place and several task forces and workshops were organized in different European cities in order for this Project to be accomplished; and, for a long period of time, we had to keep our Project protected and concealed behind or within other organizations and to apply counterintelligence methods and techniques (mainly in order to anticipate and preempt disruptions). Thus, complying with every initiatory formality of the corresponding initiatory system, I have created various types of Masonic Lodges, esoteric Colleges, and illuminist associations in order to serve as outer, protective rings of the Modern and Perfecting Rite of Symbolic Masonry during the latter's "nascent period" and to help keep the Modern and Perfecting Rite of Symbolic Masonry innocent and undefiled.

In 2022, the aforementioned Project, which started in London in 2008, came to completion with the publication of this book. By the end of 2021, I had managed to write the final draft of the Modern and Perfecting Rite of Symbolic Masonry (M∴P∴R∴S∴M∴), which is included in this book, and it has been approved by my associates in the context of the aforementioned Project. Thus, in 2022, the Autonomous Order of the Modern and Perfecting Rite of Symbolic Masonry (A∴O∴M∴P∴R∴S∴M∴) was officially founded and publicly disclosed as a robust, fully developed, strong, and independent Freemasonic subject. The old group of the "Scholarly and Political Order of the Ur-Illuminati" has reached its "telos" and, thus, it has been developed into the "Autonomous Order of the Modern and Perfecting Rite of Symbolic Masonry," just as, in the seventeenth century, Dr. John Wilkins's "Invisible College" was developed into the "Royal Society."

The Modern and Perfecting Rite of Symbolic Masonry (M∴P∴R∴S∴M∴) consists of three degrees, namely, those of an Entered Apprentice, a Fellow Craft, and a Master Mason; and I have composed rituals, lectures, and catechisms for each and every one of these three degrees (and I have written the Constitution of the Autonomous Order of the Modern and Perfecting Rite of Symbolic Masonry). By composing the aforementioned rituals, lectures, and catechisms, I have reformed Symbolic Masonry in order to achieve the following goals:

- to truly dereligionize Symbolic Masonry;

- to shift the emphasis of the rituals of Freemasonry from mythology and religious acts and narratives to philosophy and psychoanalysis;

- to defend, study, and further develop modernity (modern philosophy and modern political and economic thought);

- to institute a truly universal system of Symbolic Masonry for men and women;

- to preserve the traditional underpinnings of Symbolic Masonry that derive from ancient and medieval Operative Masonry while simultaneously integrating important elements (mainly teachings) of other Freemasonic (ultra-Craft) Orders into Symbolic Masonry in a consistent way;

- to endow Symbolic Masonry with a clearly and consistently philosophical character in accordance with my conception of Freemasonry as a system of dramatized philosophy and philosophical dramaturgy; and

- to render Symbolic Masonry capable of providing an inspiring and creative context for the conduct of thorough philosophical, theological, scientific, and political discussions, the development of interpersonal communication, and the forging of authentic fraternal relations on the basis of shared values, principles, meanings, and goals.

The Autonomous Order of the Modern and Perfecting Rite of Symbolic Masonry creates only Symbolic Masons, and it does not recognize any Masonic degree as superior to the Master Mason degree. However, the Autonomous Order of the Modern and Perfecting Rite of Symbolic Masonry has incorporated in its three degrees many significant elements and teachings of several Masonic systems of "higher degrees," such as the Ancient and Accepted Scottish Rite. Indeed, every major philosophical and political teaching of the 33 degrees of the Ancient and Accepted Scottish Rite is included in the 3 degree of the Modern and Perfecting Rite of Symbolic Masonry.

The major goal of the Autonomous Order of the Modern and Perfecting Rite of Symbolic Masonry is to preserve, protect, defend, teach, and propagate the Modern and Perfecting Rite of Symbolic Masonry internationally. The Modern and Perfecting Rite of Symbolic Masonry signifies a substantial reform of Symbolic Masonry on the basis of the following principles:

Firstly, the Modern and Perfecting Rite of Symbolic Masonry has shifted the center of gravity of Symbolic Masonry from mythology, religious texts, didactic tales, and complex rituality to philosophy, science, and psychoanalysis. For this reason, the Modern and Perfecting Rite of Symbolic Masonry is based on Operative Masonry as a source of inspiration, but it dismisses the use of religious Masonic rituals, and its ceremonies are carried out according to new Masonic dramas and catechisms based on philosophy, science, and psychoanalysis. Therefore, the Autonomous Order of the Modern and Perfecting Rite of Symbolic Masonry understands and practises Freemasonry in a way that is substantially different from the way in which the Grand Lodge of London and Westminster, the Grand Lodge of Scotland, and the Grand Lodge of Ireland formed Symbolic Masonry in the eighteenth and the nineteenth centuries.

Secondly, the Modern and Perfecting Rite of Symbolic Masonry is a genuinely universal Freemasonic Rite, and, for this reason, it is not restricted territorially to the level of national institutions, but it perceives and treats the entire world as a unified Freemasonic Jurisdiction, and it maintains the right to found Lodges and Regional Directorates of this Rite internationally. The supreme, overarching, and sovereign governing body of every Lodge and every Regional Directorate of the Modern and Perfecting Rite of Symbolic Masonry is the Grand Lodge of the Autonomous Order of the Modern and Perfecting Rite of Symbolic Masonry. Additionally, in accordance with its principle of universality, the Autonomous Order of the Modern and Perfecting Rite of Symbolic Masonry admits both men and women to membership, does not require Freemasons to declare a religious faith, and has eliminated every religious or quasi-religious practice from its ceremonies.

Thirdly, the Modern and Perfecting Rite of Symbolic Masonry is humanistic, and it endorses and promotes scholarly rigor. Its interests extend across all scholarly disciplines, namely, across the humanities, the social sciences, and the natural sciences. It is within this context that the Autonomous Order of the Modern and Perfecting Rite of Symbolic Masonry permits and encourages political and religious discussion within its Lodges. Our Order seeks to create fulfilled human beings. The great Prussian philosopher, linguist, educationalist, and diplomat Wilhelm von Humboldt has pointedly argued that the core principle and requirement of a fulfilled human being is the ability to inquire and create in a free and rational way. Thus, Humboldt promoted the concept of "holistic" academic education (in German, "Bildung"), he identified knowledge with power, and he identified education with liberty.

Finally, regarding my perseverance and rigor in dealing with demanding philosophical and scientific problems, I should mention that I presented a synthetic view of mathematics and philosophy in the dissertation that I wrote (under the supervision of Professor and Academician Themistocles M. Rassias) at the Department of Mathematics of the University of La Verne (California) and was published under the title *Topics in Mathematical Analysis and Differential Geometry* by the World Scientific Publishing Company in 1998. Moreover, the multidimensional situational and, generally, historical awareness that characterizes me has been enhanced by my professional background as a partner of the private intelligence company R-Techno Ltd specializing in political economy and socio-cultural analysis, as a Doctor of Philosophy of the *Academia Teológica de San Andrés (Ukrainian Orthodox Church in Mexico, Veracruz)*, and as a consultant in noopolitics and mathematical modelling.

Nicolas Laos, 3º M∴P∴R∴S∴M∴
Founder and Grand Master of the
Autonomous Order of the Modern and Perfecting Rite of
Symbolic Masonry
Athens, Greece, September 2022

The coat of arms of the Modern and Perfecting Rite of Symbolic Masonry: ©

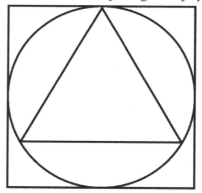

Frequent Abbreviations

In this book, I often use the following abbreviations for the sake of convenience:

A.D.C.: Assistant Director of Ceremonies
D.C.: Director of Ceremonies
E.A.: Entered Apprentice
F.C.: Fellow Craft
I.G.: Inner Guard
J.O.: Junior Overseer
M.M.: Master Mason
O.G.: Outer Guard
S.O.: Senior Overseer
V.M.: Venerable Master

Notice: Throughout this book, I follow the spelling "Kabbalah," but there also exist the following spellings: Qabal(l)ah (often preferred in the context of Western occultism) and Cabala(h) (often preferred by Christian Kabbalists, that is, in the context of Christian mysticism).

CHAPTER 1

FUNDAMENTAL CONCEPTS

The main objective of this chapter is to stimulate our fellow humans to the love of truth and science; to make them aware that truth emerges from the contact and interaction between consciousness and the world; to urge them to chisel their consciousness by means of reason and a rational interpretation of faith; and to teach the words Immanuel Kant wrote in 1784 about the Enlightenment: "Enlightenment is man's emergence from his self-imposed immaturity. Immaturity is the inability to use one's understanding without guidance from another. This immaturity is self-imposed when its cause lies not in lack of understanding, but in lack of resolve and courage to use it without guidance from another. *Sapere Aude!* [dare to know] 'Have courage to use your own understanding!' – that is the motto of enlightenment." This enlightenment is based upon systematic labor and freedom as well as upon a creative synthesis between imagination and intellectual rigor.

1.1 Philosophy and Science

The word "philosophy" derives from the Greek word "philosophīa" ("φιλοσοφία"). The ancient Greek word "philosophīa" is composed of two other ancient Greek words, namely: "phileīn" ("φιλεῖν") and "sophīa" ("σοφία"). The word "phileīn" means "to love," "to endorse," and "to be wont to do (something)," and the word "sophīa" means "wisdom." Thus, according to the etymology of the ancient Greek word "philosophīa," philosophy means love for, pursuit of, and devotion to wisdom. By the term "wisdom," we may mean a set of dispositions, skills, and policies on the basis of which one can deliberate about the relationship between consciousness and the objects to which consciousness refers, as well as, about what matters and has value in life, and act accordingly.

The verb "philosophein" ("φιλοσοφεῖν"), which means "to philosophize," was used by the ancient Greek historian Herodotus, who, in his *Histories*, 1:30:9-12, writes that Croesus, the King of Libya, entertained the Athenian philosopher, lawmaker, and poet Solon in the palace, and he addressed Solon as follows: "My Athenian guest, we have heard a lot about you because of your wisdom and of your wanderings, how as one who philosophizes [loves learning] you have travelled much of the world for the sake of understanding it."

The sixth-century B.C. Ionian Greek philosopher and mathematician Pythagoras was, arguably, the first person who invented the term "philosophy," and who called himself a "philosopher." In particular, Diogenes Laertius, in his *Lives of Eminent Philosophers* (Book VIII, Chapter 1: Pythagoras, 8) writes the following:

> Sosicrates in his *Successions of Philosophers* says that, when Leon the tyrant of Phlius asked him [namely, Pythagoras] who he was, he said, "A philosopher," and that he compared life to the Great Games, where some went to compete for the prize and others went with wares to sell, but the best as spectators; for similarly, in life, some grow up with servile natures, greedy for fame and gain, but the philosopher seeks truth.

Moreover, Diogenes Laertius, in his *Lives of Eminent Philosophers* (Book V, Chapter 1: Aristotle, 20) writes that, when Aristotle was asked what advantage he had ever gained from philosophy, Aristotle's response was the following: "This, that I do without being ordered what some are constrained to do by their fear of the law." From Aristotle's perspective, philosophy (expressing a continuous quest for knowledge, which is dialectically directed towards the ultimate knowledge) enables one to understand the underlying order and harmony of the world and, thus, to act rationally without coercion.

Plato, in his *Symposium*, 203e-204a, argues as follows:

> [...] no gods ensue wisdom or desire to be made wise; such they are already; nor does anyone else that is wise ensue it. Neither do the ignorant ensue wisdom, nor desire to be made wise: in this very point is ignorance distressing, when a person who is not comely or worthy or intelligent is satisfied with himself. The man who does not feel himself defective has no desire for that whereof he feels no defect.

From the aforementioned Platonic perspective, philosophy is the pursuit of that part of wisdom which one has not yet acquired. Therefore, according to Plato, humanity's progress in philosophy is equivalent to humanity's progress towards its ontological integration and completion. Those who do not philosophize are either totally accomplished divine beings, already possessing the entire wisdom, or ignorant persons, who are characterized by either unconscious ignorance (that is, they are unaware of what they do not know) or complacent ignorance (that is, they are intellectually idle).

In general, philosophers are preoccupied with methodic and systematic investigations of the problems that originate from the reference of consciousness to the world and to itself. In other words, philosophers are preoccupied with the problems that originate from humanity's attempt to articulate a qualitative interpretation of the integration of the consciousness of existence into the reality of the world. The aforementioned problems pertain to the world itself, to consciousness, and to the relation between consciousness and the world.

It goes without saying that scientists are also preoccupied with similar problems. However, there are two important differences between philosophy and science. Firstly, from the perspective of science, it suffices to find and formulate relations and laws (generalizations) that – under certain conditions and to some extent – can interpret the objects of scientific research, whereas philosophy moves beyond these findings and formulations in order to evaluate the objects of philosophical research, and, thus, ultimately, to articulate a *general method* and a *general criterion* for the explanation of every object of philosophical research. Whereas sciences consist of images and explanations of these images, philosophies are formulated by referring to wholes and by inducing wholes from parts. Hence, for instance, a philosopher will ask what is "scientific" about science, namely, what is the true meaning of science? Therefore, philosophy and science differ from each other with regard to the level of generality that characterizes their endeavors. Secondly, as the French philosopher Pierre Hadot has pointed out, philosophy – unlike the various scientific disciplines – is not merely a science, but it is a "way of life," and, specifically, philosophy signifies a conscious being's free and deliberate decision to seek truth for the sake of knowledge itself, since a philosopher is aware that knowledge is inextricably linked to the existential freedom and the ontological integration and completion of the human being.[1]

---

1   Pierre Hadot, *Philosophy As a Way of Life*, edited by Arnold I. Davidson, Oxford: Blackwell, 1995.

Beyond the similarities between philosophy and science, philosophy is an impetus for the creation of a world of meanings (in Greek, "noēmata") that express human creativity. Moving beyond those approaches that understand "meaning" as a constituent element of language, Edmund Husserl used the Greek term "nōema" (plural: "noēmata") to designate the intentional object, namely, that element due to which an intention of the human being – such as one's intention to say something, to move one's hand, etc. – acquires content and becomes significant. In particular, in his book *Ideas: General Introduction to Pure Phenomenology*, where he introduced the Greek term "nōema" (meaning "thought," or "what is thought about"), Husserl argued that any conscious experience is directed towards an object, and that, corresponding to all points in "the manifold data of the real (*reelle*) noetic content, there is a variety of data displayable in really pure (*wirklicher reiner*) intuition, and in a correlative 'noematic content,' or briefly 'noema.'"[2] Every intentional act has noematic content, or briefly "nōema," which is a mental act-process (such as an act of judging, meaning, liking, etc.) that is directed towards the intentionally held object (such as, the judged as judged, the meant as meant, the liked as liked, etc.). In other words, every intentional act has, as part of its formation, a correlative "nōema," which is the object of the act.[3]

Ontology is the branch of philosophy that is concerned with the study of being, which is the most abstract concept. "Being" is a self-sufficient reality that is sustained either by being a closed system or by being an open system. According to the terminology of modern philosophy, all ontological theories can be divided into two categories: "philosophical realism" and "idealism." In other words, according to modern philosophical terminology, there are two general models whereby philosophers interpret the world: one gives primacy to the reality of the world, and it is known as philosophical realism, whereas the other gives primacy to the reality of consciousness, and it is known as philosophical idealism.

1.2 Knowledge

Knowledge is an intellectual function according to which one constantly considers that an object corresponds to reality. Knowledge presupposes a correspondence between thing and intellect. This argument has been put forward by Aristotle in his *Metaphysics* 1011b25 as follows: "To say of what is that it is not, or of what is not that it is, is false,

---

2   Edmund Husserl, *Ideas: General Introduction to Pure Phenomenology*, edited by W. R. Boyce Gibson, New York: Collier Books, 1962, p. 238.

3   Ibid, p. 229.

while to say of what is that it is, and of what is not that it is not, is true," and virtually identical assertions can be found in Plato (*Cratylus* 385b2, *Sophist* 263b).

At the level of rational understanding, corresponding to the mental process used in thinking and perceiving, consciousness plays an active role, whose manifestation is reason. In his seminal book *Critique of Pure Reason*, Immanuel Kant, who was arguably the most important representative of the European Enlightenment, explained that "reason" is an *a priori*, that is, pre-experiential, structure in the context of which various categories are interrelated, and, whenever they are adequately activated, they can connect isolated empirical data with each other, thus making possible the formulation of synthetic judgments, though which one can creatively transcend the level of experience and ascend to a level of rational understanding.

One of the major goals of philosophy is to identify and study the relations between consciousness and external reality. The various relations that can be conceived with respect to consciousness and external reality are reducible to two general philosophical models: realism and idealism. In general, philosophical realism consists in the following thesis: since experience provides consciousness with images of a reality that seems to be external to our minds, it naturally follows that this reality is the cause that generates the set of the given partial images, and, therefore, according to the principle of causality – a mind-independent reality exists necessarily. Whereas the representatives of realism emphasize the principle of causality, the representatives of idealism emphasize the principle of identity. In other words, according to idealism, the nature of consciousness and the nature of external reality are neither totally different from each other nor contrary to each other. Idealists view the world not as something reflected in consciousness, but as an extension and a projection of consciousness outside of itself and also as consciousness itself.

The main epistemological debates revolve around the following "schools" of thought:

Empiricism: it is the view that the only grounds for justified belief are those that rest ultimately on observation. Based on the philosophies of David Hume and John Locke, the central empiricist premise is that science must be based on a phenomenalist nominalism, that is, the notion that only statements that refer to observable phenomena are cognitively significant and that any statements that do not refer to independent atomized objects cannot be granted the status of justified knowledge.[4] According to empiricism, science can be founded on a bedrock of such objective sense data ("pure observation"), and from this bedrock can be established, by induction, the entire structure of science.

But empiricism has the following defects: (i) The epistemological warrant offered by empiricism is very narrow, because it is based on direct observation, and, therefore, it rules out any consideration of (unobservable) things, such as social structures, or even social facts (which, according to the French sociologist Émile Durkheim, refer to those shared social concepts and understandings such as crime, which he argued that should be treated as "things"). Hence, a strict variety of empiricism actually offers a very narrow-minded and restrictive understanding of "reality." (ii) Empiricism does not allow us to talk about "causes," since these are unobservable. In the context of empiricism, causation is reduced to mere correlation, and our inquiry is therefore limited to that of "prediction" and cannot involve "explanation." (iii) The kind of pure unvarnished perception requested by empiricists is impossible. John Searle has pointed out that subjectivity is an essential characteristic of conscious states,[5] and W. V. O. Quine has pointed out that theory is involved in all empirical observation, thus making absolute objectivism impossible.[6] Furthermore, both Immanuel Kant and Gestalt Psychology[7] have pointed out that the conscious mind plays a much more active role in perception than the one thought by empiricists.

Rationalism: it is based on the philosophies of René Descartes, Gottfried Wilhelm Leibniz, and Baruch Spinoza, and it has been the historical counterpoint to Hume's and Locke's empiricism. Rationalism was very much influenced by the scientific revolution of Newton, Kepler, and Galileo, and, thus, it has subscribed to the view that the kinds of mechanisms discovered by the previous natural scientists were quite different kinds

---

4   Leszek Kolakowski, *Positivist Philosophy*, Harmondsworth: Penguin Books, 1972, pp. 11-17.

5   John Searle, *The Rediscovery of the Mind*, Cambridge, Mass.: MIT Press, 1992.

6   W. V. O. Quine, "Two Dogmas of Empiricism", in: W.V.O. Quine, ed., *From a Logical Point of View*, 2nd edition, Cambridge, MA: Harvard University Press, 1961, p. 20-46.

7   Gestalt Psychology was founded by Max Wertheimer (1880-1943). Wertheimer noted that we perceive motion where there is nothing more than a rapid sequence of individual sensory events. This argument is based on observations that he made with his stroboscope at the Frankfurt train station and on additional observations that he made in his laboratory when he experimented with lights flashing in rapid succession (like the Christmas lights that appear to course around the tree, or the fancy neon signs in Las Vegas that seem to move). Wertheimer called this effect "apparent motion," and it is actually the basic principle of motion pictures. According to Wertheimer, apparent motion proves that people don't respond to isolated segments of sensation but to the whole (*Gestalt*) of the situation. See: Wolfgang Köhler, *Gestalt Psychology*, New York: Liveright, 1992.

of things to those which people can observe. In other words, rationalists stress that perception or observation is never sufficient on its own, and it requires logical processing. The central rationalist premise is that the senses cannot give us an understanding of the mechanisms that generate the observables we perceive and that the notion of logic, which is a property of the human intellect, can work out the relationship between observables and deduce the causal mechanisms at work. We can only gain knowledge of the world by using logic in order to process/explain what we observe or experience. This notion of rationality, with mathematics as the exemplar, was based on a foundation of certain truth, which for Descartes was an intuitive truth known by all minds; thus he declared *"cogito ergo sum"* ("I think therefore I am"): reflective minds could doubt everything, except they could not doubt that they were thinking, and this provides the basis for secure knowledge about the world.

It goes without saying that the knowledge provided by rationalism is qualitatively far superior to the knowledge provided by empiricism. But rationalism, at least in its early formative stage, has the following defects: (i) There is more than one kind of rationality, if, in Cartesian spirit, we take it to mean a deductive system based on intuitive axioms. Different individuals might claim that their intuitions were different from those of others. For instance, Descartes claimed that Euclidean geometry was absolute, being based on definitive axioms, but Riemann, Lobachevsky, and other mathematicians have created non-Euclidean geometries, based on different intuitive axioms. Moreover, N. A. Vasiliev, Jan Łukasiewicz, Hans Reichenbach, A. H. S. Korzybski, Lotfi Zadeh, R. A. Wilson and other logicians have created various non-Aristotelian logics, based on different intuitive axioms. (ii) The human being relates to beings and things in the world through significances that one assigns to them,[8] and, therefore, the fundamental significations (specifically, the values) that underpin human action must explicitly find their position in every meaningful discussion about social systems.

Pragmatism: it is based on the philosophies of William James, Charles Pierce, and John Dewey, and it attempts to combine the rationalist thesis that the mind is always active in interpreting experience and observation with the empiricist thesis that revisions in our beliefs are to be made as a result of experience.[9] According to pragmatism, theories are underdeter-

8   Ernst Cassirer, *The Philosophy of Symbolic Forms*, Volume One: Language, Volume Two: Mythical Thought, translated by R. Manheim, New Haven: Yale University Press, 1955.
9   For a general introduction to pragmatism, see for instance: C. J. Misak, ed., *Pragmatism*,

mined by the evidence, and, therefore, scientists have to choose between a number of theories that may all be compatible with the available evidence. Hence, as William James has argued, truth is "only the expedient in the way of belief," meaning that we need to adjust our ideas as to what is true as experience unfolds. Pragmatism, then, defines what is true as what is most useful in the way of belief (thus, giving rise to a utilitarian epistemology).

However, pragmatism is ultimately self-defeating. Even though pragmatism appears to reflect a dynamic attitude towards reality and epistemology and to be a progressive epistemological stance, it is deeply conservative and assigns a deeply passive role to human consciousness. By stressing the adaptation of our ideas to an unfolding experience, pragmatists ignore the dynamic continuity between the reality of the world and the reality of consciousness, a dynamic continuity that allows conscious beings to impose their intentionality on reality, instead of merely adapting to a reality that is external to their consciousness. Conscious beings are not merely obliged to look for methods of adaptation to reality, but they can utilize and restructure reality according to their intentionality.

Scientific realism: it is based on the philosophies of Roy Bhaskar[10] and Rom Harré.[11] The central premise of scientific realism is that it makes sense to talk of a world outside of experience. Thus, scientific realism is primarily concerned with the uncovering of the structures and things of an objective scientific cosmos. Scientific realism treats theoretical concepts, specifically, "ideas," such as electrons or sets, in the same way as so-called "facts," and, therefore, it argues that the empiricist conception of the role of theories (as heuristic) is wrong. Bhaskar distinguishes among the real, the actual and the empirical: the first refers to what entities and mechanisms make up the world, the second to events, and the third to that which we experience. According to Bhaskar, empiricism makes the mistake of looking at the third of these as a way of explaining the other two so that it reduces ontological questions to epistemological questions. Furthermore, Bhaskar rejects rationalism, too, by arguing that it too reduces ontology to epistemology by its reliance on theoretically necessary conceptual truths to explain the world. In contrast to empiricism and rationalism, realist science is an attempt to describe and explain structures

Calgary: University of Calgary Press, 1999.
10   Roy Bhaskar, *A Realist Theory of Science*, Brighton: Harvester, 1978.
11   Rom Harré, *Varieties of Realism*, Oxford: Blackwell, 1986.

and processes of the world that exist independently of human consciousness.

On the other hand, P. M. M. Duhem has made the following critical observations, which together are known as the "underdetermination of theory by data," and demonstrate the weaknesses of scientific realism: a hypothesis cannot be used to derive testable predictions in isolation, but "auxiliary" assumptions, such as background theories, hypotheses about instruments and measurements, etc., are also necessary, and, therefore, if subsequent observations and experiments produce data that conflict with those predicted, it is no simple matter to identify where the error lies; different, conflicting theories may be consistent with the same data, and, since the theories differ precisely in what they say about the unobservable (given that their observable consequences – the data – are all shared), the choice of which theory to believe is *underdetermined* by the data.[12]

Phenomenology, Structuralism, and Hermeneutics: For Edmund Husserl,[13] phenomenology is a method according to which the researcher focuses on the essential structures that allow the objects that are taken for granted in the "natural attitude" (which is characteristic of both our everyday life and ordinary science) to "constitute themselves" in consciousness. Phenomenology is characterized by subjectivism in the sense that phenomenological inquiries are initially directed, in Cartesian fashion, towards consciousness and its presentations. On the other hand, phenomenology is not characterized by any psychological or mentalistic forms of subjectivism, since the subject-matter of phenomenology is not the realm of psychological ideas affirmed by empiricism but rather the ideal meanings and universal relations with which consciousness is confronted in its experience.

The phenomenological method comes from a position prior to reflexive thought, called pre-reflexive thought, which consists of a turn to the very things. At that moment, the phenomenologist holds a phenomenological stance that enables one to keep oneself open enough to live that experience in its wholeness, preventing any judgment from interfering with one's openness to the description. The phenomenologist is not concerned with the particular elements of the object under investigation, but

---

12   Pierre Maurice Marie Duhem, *The Aim and Structure of Physical Theory*, Princeton, NJ: Princeton University Press, 1954.
13   See: Herbert Spiegelberg, *The Phenomenological Movement*, third revised and enlarged edition, The Hague: Nijhoff, 1982; Elisabeth Ströker, *Husserl's Transcendental Phenomenology*, Stanford: Stanford University Press, 1993.

with the given object's ideal essence that is hidden by and shines through the particulars. Husserl used the term *"epoché" (suspension of judgment)* to refer to the purification of experience of its factuality.

In his preface to *Ideas Pertaining to a Pure Phenomenology – First Book: General Introduction to a Pure Phenomenology*, Husserl argues that phenomenology, like mathematics, is "the science of pure possibilities" which "must everywhere precede the science of real facts." By bracketing factuality, phenomenology exerted important influence on existentialism, and, in fact, it became the method of existentialism,[14] which is based on the thesis that consciousness attributes meaning to the reality of the world. In contrast to Aristotle's philosophy – which assigns primary significance to the essence of things (namely, to the attribute or set of attributes that make an object what it fundamentally is, and which it has by necessity, and without which it loses its identity) – the philosophers of existence, such as S. A. Kierkegaard, Martin Heidegger and J.-P. Sartre, argue that what is ontologically significant is not the essence of being but the presence of being, that is, its existence.

The next major step in the development of the phenomenological method took place when it was applied to the investigation of those elements of reality whose knowledge is prior to the knowledge of the essence of reality, specifically, when it was applied to the investigation of the elements that constitute the structure of reality. By the term "structure," we mean an internal reality that is governed by each own order, which it creates and recreates by itself. In other words, a structure consists of the fundamental rules that govern the behavior and the relations of the members of a system (a "system" being a set endowed with a structure). The method of structuralism is the final stage of phenomenology's attempt to cope with the problems that arise from the philosophical investigation of the meaning of reality. Additionally, structuralism corroborates Gaston Bachelard's argument that there is a dynamic continuity between knowing consciousness and known object.[15]

Closely related to the project of investigating the meaning of reality is Hans-Georg Gadamer's method of hermeneutics. Its central premise is anti-naturalist in that it does not see the social world as in any sense amenable to the empiricist and especially the positivist epistemology. Hermeneutics, having developed out of textual analysis, emphasizes the difference between the analysis of nature ("explanation") and the analysis

---

14   See: Haim Gordon, *Dictionary of Existentialism*, New York: Greenwood Press, 1999; Thomas Flynn, *Existentialism: A Very Short Introduction*, Oxford: Oxford University Press, 2006.
15   See: Mary Tiles, *Bachelard: Science and Objectivity*, Cambridge: Cambridge University Press, 1984.

of the mind ("understanding"). Karl Jaspers[16] defines the scientific analysis of "objective causal connections" as "explaining" ("Erklären"), whereas he designates the "understanding of psychic events 'from within'" as "understanding" ("Verstehen"). In this way, Jaspers's thought opened the philosophical path to Gadamer's hermeneutics.

According to hermeneutics, we can only understand the world by our being caught up in a system of significance. Persons analyze and act within what Gadamer[17] refers to as an "horizon," by which he means their beliefs, preconceptions, and, in general, their embeddedness in the particular history and culture that shaped them. Thus, from the viewpoint of hermeneutics, the notions of truth and reason are consequences of humanity's embeddedness in systems of significance (value systems). Epistemology, hence, can never be something prior to or independent of culture and has to be seen as secondary to ontology.

In summary, the study of phenomenology, structuralism, and hermeneutics, leads us to the awareness that the transition from the natural sciences to the social sciences is an upward-moving process known as "*emergentism.*" Therefore, the journey in the opposite direction, downward, which might justify "*reductionism,*" is not valid. Thus, all forms of reductionism are discarded. The specific nature of sociology clearly emerges when we examine it from an ontological point of view. We then *see* that social reality presents different characteristics from the realities of biology and physics. Social reality is *a human creation.* It exists as long as the humans who created it believe in it. It ceases to exist when no one believes in it any longer. In his book *Le Regole dell'Azione Sociale (Milano: Il Saggiatore, 1983), Giuliano Di Bernardo* (specifically, in the chapter entitled "La fondazione del sociale") shows that social reality is constructed by humanity through "*constitutive rules.*" In particular, Di Bernardo (ibid) maintains that, based on constitutive rules, language, and the collective self, social reality has a dual ontology: one that is "*visible,*" observable, made up of objects from the external world, such as houses, monuments, and money, and another that is "*invisible,*" made up, for instance, of housing regulations, the aesthetics of monuments, and the significance of money. Hence, all ontologies of social reality must be based on both these visible and invisible aspects. The visible aspect is similar to the ontology of physics and biology, whereas the invisible aspect, which cannot be reduced to physics and biology, is the "*specific quality*" of sociology.

---

16   See: P. A. Schilpp, ed., *The Philosophy of Karl Jaspers*, New York: Tudor Publishing Company, 1957.

17   H.-G. Gadamer, *Truth and Method*, London: Sheed and Ward, 1975.

Critical Theory: it was developed out the work of the Frankfurt School in the inter-war years,[18] and its most influential thinker has been Jürgen Habermas. Habermas has put forward the thesis that there are three types of knowledge:[19] empirical-analytical (the natural sciences), histori-cal-hermeneutic (concerned with meaning and understanding), and crit-ical sciences (concerned with emancipation). According to Habermas, each of these types of knowledge has its own set of "cognitive interests," respectively: those of a technical interest in control and prediction, a prac-tical interest in understanding, and an emancipatory interest in enhancing freedom. From the viewpoint of the Critical School, there can be so such thing as true (interest-free) empirical statements (e.g., in the realm of the natural sciences independent of the knowledge-constitutive interest in control and prediction).

However, in the late 1960s, Habermas moved away from the above-mentioned rather restricted notion of knowledge/constitutive in-terests towards the development of what he calls a theory of communica-tive action.[20] Thus, his epistemology is based on the notion of discourse ethics or universal pragmatics, according to which knowledge emerges out of a consensus theory of truth. Central to his epistemology is his idea of an "ideal speech situation," which he sees as implicit in the act of communication and as rationally entailing moral and normative commit-ments. The "ideal speech situation"[21] is based on the notion that acts of communication necessarily presuppose that statements are: (i) compre-hensible, (ii) true, (iii) right, and (iv) sincere.

Habermas is aware that the ideal speech situation is something that is not commonly found in communicative actions, but he believes that we could in principle reach a consensus on the validity of the previous four claims, and that this consensus would be achieved if we envisaged a situ-ation in which coercive power and distortion were removed from com-munication so that the "force of the better argument prevails."[22] Hence, Habermas, following Kantianism, seeks to avoid the simple objectivism of elementary positivism whilst at the same time refusing to endorse the kind of relativism implicit in traditional hermeneutics.

---

18   David Held, *Introduction to Critical Theory*, Berkeley, CA: University of California Press, 1980.
19   Jürgen Habermas, *Knowledge and Human Interests*, Cambridge: Polity, 1987 (first pub-lished 1968).
20   Jürgen Habermas, *The Theory of Communicative Action, Vol. 2: The Critique of Functional-ist Reason*, Cambridge: Polity, 1987.
21   See: William Outhwaite, *Habermas: A Critical Introduction*, Cambridge: Polity, 1994, p. 40.
22   Ibid, p. 40.

Rational dynamicity: My studies in the aforementioned philosophical "schools" have led me to the conclusion that, even though the reality of the world is not a projection of human consciousness, it can, nevertheless, under certain conditions, be utilized and restructured by the intentionality of human consciousness. I have called this thesis "rational dynamicity." My notion of rational dynamicity, contra realism and idealism, implies that the reality of the world and the reality of consciousness are not one, but they are united with each other. Therefore, rational dynamicity recognizes and respects the "otherness" of the reality of the world, but, simultaneously, it underpins one's historical action in order to impose one's intentionality on the reality of the world.

My notion of rational dynamicity stems from the synthesis between structuralism and hermeneutics. By resorting to the analysis of the rational dynamicity of consciousness, we can interpret both ontological reality and the intentionality of consciousness, which imposes its own structures on ontological reality in order to utilize ontological reality. As a criterion of reality and action, rational dynamicity derives from consciousness, but (since it is not intended to offer philosophical "legitimacy" to arbitrary idealistic action) it is activated only when it is possible to be applied to objective reality. Additionally, the method of rational dynamicity is based on the ontological position that objective reality is activated for, that is, made present in, consciousness when consciousness assigns meaning and significance to objective reality. Even though reality is multidimensional, it becomes significant for consciousness only when it becomes mentally updated in relation to the intentionality of consciousness. Therefore, the knowledge of reality that is based on the method of rational dynamicity is in agreement with both the nature of consciousness and the nature of reality.

If the structure of the world were totally different from the structure of consciousness, then the latter would be unable to gain even partial knowledge of the reality of the world (it could only know itself). If the reality of the world were merely a projection of human consciousness, that is, if the reality of the world were identified with the contents of human consciousness, then consciousness would not try so hard to know the world, and the knowledge of the world would be identified with the knowledge of the self. Thus, neither realism nor idealism can stand as a general theory of reality. Rational dynamicity implies that there is a dynamic continuity between the reality of the world and the reality of consciousness. Therefore, the study of any institution must be focused on the analysis of the relationship between the reality of the world as a repository of opportunities and the reality of consciousness as a repository of intentions.

1.3 Religion

By the term "God," in general, people refer to the ultimate, transcendent source of the meaning of the beings and things that exist in the world. Religions are means by which people seek to connect with God. My studies in the philosophy of religion[23] have led me to the conclusion that we can distinguish the following four categories of religion:

> • *Instinctive religion:* this is the most primitive type of religion. The origins of religion lie at the very beginnings of history, from when *Homo sapiens* first appeared and was faced with a strange, often hostile environment and a mysterious, almost incomprehensible existence. Early humans encountered vast forces, upon which they were totally dependent, and yet which were outside humanity's control, such as: the sun, the moon, the forces of nature, the movement of the animals, and the growth of the plants. Moreover, in their own lives, people were faced with mysterious and powerful forces, namely, birth, death, sickness, thirst, and hunger. It was in search of an explanation for, and the ability to exercise some control over, these powers that humans developed the first type of religion, which I call instinctive religion.
>
> What they could not control physically (for instance, the movement of the seasons, or the fertility of the herds) they tried to fathom and manipulate symbolically in rituals. In addition, they developed myths to explain what things were and how they came to be. The most important evolutionary advantage that instinctive religion offered to humanity was the management of existential anxiety and the rationalization of the cosmos. However, in the course of their explorations, humans also stumbled onto some rudiments of science, and, therefore, they started developing astronomy (at first as astrology), chemistry, medicine (in herbalism and later alchemy), and other scientific disciplines. Furthermore, gradually, people started exploring their own natures and social life, and, therefore, they started developing an elementary psychology and an elementary sociology. As people's adaptation to and control of the environment increased, as their dependence on the forces of nature lessened, and as new problems of a psychological and sociological nature began to preoccupy humanity more and more, religion became more speculative and less concerned with the everyday needs of survival.

---

23   See: Immanuel Kant, *Religion and Rational Theology*, translated and edited by Allen W. Wood and George Di Giovanni, Cambridge: Cambridge University Press, 2001; Ludwig Feuerbach, *The Essence of Religion*, translated by Alexander Loos, New York: Prometheus Books, 2004; Max Weber, *The Sociology of Religion*, translated by Ephraim Fischoff, Boston: Beacon, 1993.

- *Speculative religion:* The most important founders of speculative religion are Akhenaten (the Egyptian pharaoh-creator of monotheism), Confucius, Zoroaster, Gautama Buddha, Moses, Hermes Trismegistus (a mythical personification rather than a person), Socrates, Plato, Jesus of Nazareth, and Muhammad ibn Abdullah. The most important evolutionary advantage that speculative religion offered to humanity was the cultivation of moral consciousness and the rationalization of social life. Moral consciousness, which is the consciousness of existence itself when it operates as a judge. Moral consciousness is a function of the following variables: sentiments, volition, and reason. Sentiments are emotions equipped with judgments, and, therefore, they are the strongest underpinnings of moral consciousness, since they can help moral consciousness to make decisions even when one's will falters and/or when one's intellect is irresolute. Volition is guided by the principle of pleasure, which expresses attraction to life. Reason expresses the power of consciousness to control itself. It is important to mention that, as moral consciousness develops more and more, there arises an increasing tendency to *specify* morality, in the sense that moral rules tend to be increasingly differentiated from religion and law, and the moral subject recognizes human consciousness as the source of moral values.

- *Ancient mystery cults:* this is an intermediate stage in the transition from instinctive religion to the most advanced forms of speculative religion. Thus, ancient mystery cults combined the rituality of instinctive religion with the philosophical pursuits of speculative religion.[24]

- *Superstitious religion:* this is a degenerate category of religions. Superstitious religions are instruments of manipulation and oppression of the masses by forces of spiritual and political despotism.[25]

1.4 Esotericism

The term "esotericism" is controversial and is often confused with the colloquial adjectival sense of something that is obscure and technical or that pertains to the minutiae of a particular area of common knowledge. The term esotericism derives from the Greek root "eso," which means inner. Plato, in his dialogue *Alcibiades*, uses the expression "ta eso," meaning the inner things, and, in his dialogue *Theaetetus*, he uses the expression "ta exo," meaning "the outside things." The Greek adjective "esoterikos" (eso-

---

24   See: Walter Burkert, *Ancient Mystery Cults*, Cambridge, Mass.: Harvard University Press, 1987.
25   See: Arthur Versluis, *The New Inquisitions: Heretic-Hunting and the Intellectual Origins of Modern Totalitarianism*, Oxford: Oxford University Press, 2006.

teric) was coined by the rhetorician and satirist Lucian of Samosata (second century A.D.) in his book *The Auction of Lives* (paragraph 26). The term "esoteric" first appeared in English in Thomas Stanley's *History of Philosophy*, which was published in 1701. Thomas Stanley used the term "esoteric" in order to describe the mystery-school of Pythagoras, since the Pythagoreans were divided into the exoteric circle (under training) and the esoteric circle (admitted into the 'inner' circle). The corresponding noun "esotericism" was coined by the French philosopher and historian Jacques Matter in his book *Histoire Critique Du Gnosticisme* (1828), and it was popularized by the nineteenth century French occult author and ceremonial magician Eliphas Lévi (born Alphonse Louis Constant).

One of the most influential attempts to explain what unites the various currents designated by "esotericism" in the scholarly sense is due to the prominent French scholar Antoine Faivre, who held a chair in the École Pratique des Hautes Études at the Sorbonne, he was University Professor of Germanic Studies at the University of Haute-Normandie, and he was the director of the *Cahiers de l'hermétisme* and of the *Bibliothèque de l'hermétisme*. Faivre's definition of esotericism is based on his argument that the following four essential characteristics are present in the esoteric currents[26]: (i) a theory of correspondences among all parts of the invisible and the visible cosmos, (ii) the conviction that nature is a living entity owing to a divine presence or life-force, (iii) the need for mediating elements (e.g., symbols, rituals, angels, visions) in order to access spiritual knowledge, and (iv) an experience of personal and spiritual transmutation when arriving at this inner knowledge. However, the aforementioned definition of esotericism is mainly descriptive, since it refers to particular types of behavior, but it says nothing about the final causes of the different esoteric types of behavior. Thus, Faivre's definition is not as general as Faivre and his followers assert, and it tends to limit esotericism to particular esoteric types of behavior (belief systems and spiritual practices), instead of offering a broad understanding of the motives that underpin the manifestation of such behaviors. In this book, I shall follow a teleological approach to the concept of esotericism, in order to articulate a general definition of esotericism. My argument is that – if one wants to avoid the risks of lapsing into intellectual atavism and of fixating esotericists on particular stages of humanity's spiritual development – esotericism should be studied as a dynamic cultural phenomenon and, specifically, as an expression of hu-

---

26   Antoine Faivre, *Access to Western Esotericism*, New York: State University of New York Press, 1994.

manity's attempt to know oneself, to discern oneself from the world and to impose one's intentionality on the world.

Consequently, I maintain that esotericism as such, namely, the essence of esotericism (apart from the differences between particular esoteric "schools" and currents), consists in bearing witness to the reality of the human being and, in particular, to the autonomy of humanity, by focusing on the power of the intentionality of human consciousness and on the submissiveness of external reality to the intentionality of human consciousness. Additionally, the dynamic continuity between the structure of the world and the structure of human consciousness is the truth that underpins the grand synthesis between philosophy, science, and esotericism, which I propose in this book. Thus, following the previous trans-dogmatic and, indeed, a-dogmatic and teleological approach to esotericism, I understand esotericism as a program of personality creation and humanity's spiritual emancipation and as a Promethean rising of human consciousness, which can be expressed in many different ways – such as: ceremonial magic, art, science, philosophy, religion, etc.

According to the rationale that I follow in this book, esotericism is based on the thesis that every object of consciousness exists not only in itself but also inextricably united with the meaning that is attributed to it by consciousness. Therefore, every manipulation of the meanings that are attributed to things and make the world meaningful is equivalent to a manipulation of the reality of the world itself by consciousness. This is, according to my rationale, the ultimate "secret" of esotericism's power and significance. Furthermore, inherent in my previous argument is a powerful political message, since the moral autonomy that is achieved through and underpinned by my interpretation of the Western esotericism implies a high level of personal and social autonomy.

In order to place the study of esotericism within a philosophically and scientifically rigorous framework and in order to avoid charlatanism and spiritually sterile speculation, we must study esotericism as a cultural phenomenon. Hence, we must clarify two more concepts – namely, civilization and culture. From a broad perspective, the concept of civilization includes the concept of culture, but, from a narrower perspective, "civilization" can be differentiated from "culture" on the basis of the argument that "civilization" consists of the means by which consciousness tries to achieve for itself better terms for its adaptation to the world as well as of the results of the aforementioned conscious activity, whereas "culture" is the result of humanity's reflection on one's life. Civilization is a structure that consists of technology and institutions. On the other hand, culture is a reflective attitude towards institutions and an attempt to transcend institutions through myth, whose complex structure reflects the structure of institutions. In fact, "myth"[27] is the spiritual core of the elements of civilization, and, therefore, it should be clearly distinguished from the notion of a tale. The creation of tales is an unsuccessful attempt to satisfy humans' quest for an inspiring and spiritually life-giving myth. In other words, tales are spiritually puny substitutes for myth. Myth is the most important manifestation and the core of culture. Myth translates experienced reality into a symbolic language, and, in this way, it underpins the participation of a community of conscious beings in the same experience and understanding of reality.

Myth, as we have inherited it from Plato's philosophy and the ancient Mysteries, gives life to ideas. From the perspective of mythology, knowledge is not derived from static representation, but it constitutes an itinerary of the entire human being towards truth. Thus, in his dialogues *Gorgias* and *Republic*, Plato argues that "paideia" (namely, classical Greek education) consists in a transition from "doxa" (namely, a belief, unrelated to reason, that resides in the unreasoning, lower-parts of the soul) to the real being. A philosophical myth is not merely an intellectual method of teaching because it elucidates not only the significance of its subject-matter but also the content of its mythological subject-matter. Thus, a myth is not an allegory, but it is a symbol: in contrast to an allegory, a myth does not simply refer to something else, but it also discloses the significance of that "else" to which it refers. Additionally, in contrast to the analytical method, the mythological method of seeking truth consists in entering into the thing, that is, in knowing its significance, rather than going around it from the outside.

The primary purpose of civilization is to exert control over untamed forces and, hence, to transform them into forces that are controlled by human consciousness in order, ultimately, to harmonize all controlled forces with each other and with human reason. Human reason, under its different manifestations – namely, technical, scientific, and moral ones – oversees the successive phases of civilization and evaluates them according to its own dispositions. The dispositions of human reason are subject to change according to the manner in which each society understands its needs. In general, irrespective of whether a civilization gives primacy to materialistic pursuits or to more spiritual pursuits, the essence of "civili-

---

27   See: C. G. Jung, "The Relations Between the Ego and the Unconscious," in: J. Campbell, ed., *The Portable Jung*, New York: Penguin Books, 1971; Claude Lévi-Strauss, *The Raw and the Cooked*, translated by John and Doreen Weightman, Chicago: The University of Chicago Press, 1969.

zation" consists in the objectivation of the intentionality of consciousness through the construction of technological systems (e.g., machines, tools, etc.) and through institutions, whereas the essence of "culture" consists in the objectivation of the intentionality of consciousness through artistic creation, philosophy, and scientific theories and models. However, civilization and culture are neither contradictory nor incompatible to each other. Even though civilization corresponds to "technical construction" while culture corresponds to "spiritual creation," culture is embodied in civilization and underpins civilization, and, in its turn, civilization underpins the integration of culture into history.

In terms of civilization, the progress of humanity consists in the technological and institutional progress of society. On the other hand, in terms of culture, the progress of humanity is evaluated according to the spiritual deepening of the human being. Thus, as Christopher Bamford has argued, two powerful motives weave beneath the surface of the West's spiritual history: the desire to understand and the desire to love.[28]

1.5 Ideology

The term "ideology" was first formulated by the French aristocrat and philosopher Destutt de Tracy in 1796, to denote a systematic critical and (intellectually) therapeutic (or corrective) study of the sensory bases of ideas (see: George Lichtheim, *The Concept of Ideology, and Other Essays*, New York: Random House, 1967). In the most general way, we can define "ideology" as a pattern (recurring module) of symbolically invested beliefs and expressions that determine the way in which consciousness perceives, interprets, and evaluates the world in order, according to its intentionality, to formulate, mobilize, direct, organize, and justify specific ways or guiding axes of action and to reject others. In this light, ideology provides a coherent system of ideas that forms the basis of the historical action of the bearer of the corresponding ideology, and, therefore, ideology prevents intellectual squinting and ensures the stability of the strategic orientation of thought and action.

On the other hand, ideology may not always function as a coherent system of ideas that ensures the stability of the strategic orientation of thought and action, but it may degenerate into a system of ideas that overemphasizes, in an obsessive and arbitrary way, their importance in the constitution and transformation of reality. In particular, in its degenerate

---

28   Christopher Bamford, *An Endless Trace: The Passionate Pursuit of Wisdom in the West*, New York: Codhill Press, 2003.

version, the term "ideology" denotes a deficit of realism that results from self-delusion or the interest of the ideologue, who, in this case, is the representative of a prejudiced social type or collective subject and acts as a propagandist (whether or not one is aware of this situation). Hence, the degenerate version of ideology can be called obsession, which is a psychiatric condition, or, in Karl Marx's terminology, "false consciousness."

In the present book, I argue that concepts are not mere reflections of some relations that exist in the world, but they are also a peculiar factor in these relations. Ideas are facts, while concepts are social constructions that give meaning to ideological systems. Ideological systems are collective products that embody, to a greater or lesser extent, widespread concepts. As I mentioned above, ideologies (in their non-degenerate version) are not an illusory consciousness, but they are political thought, which is part of social and political reality.

The most important ways in which the ideological phenomenon manifested itself in the context of modernity are the following:

- **The ideology of bourgeois-liberalism:** Feudalism, the dominant system in medieval Europe, was a system characterized by a rigid social stratification, according to which everyone had a rigidly instituted position within an "organic whole," whose major constituent components were the class of the feudal lords, the class of the serfs, and the Church, whose major social role was to maintain a balance between the feudal lords and the serfs through religion. By the late Middle Ages, the bourgeois class (namely, a social class of professionals who were neither feudal lords nor serfs) deprecated the political, economic, and spiritual despotism of the feudal system, it revolted against feudalism, and it proclaimed that the social position of an individual should not be determined by feudal institutions, but it should be freely determined by individual action and by the interaction between individuals in the context of a free and fair society. The origins of modern liberalism can be seen most clearly in the thinking and politics linked to the English Revolution of 1688, specifically, in British empiricism and constitutionalism. The principles of constitutionalism, religious toleration, and commercial activity, which were promoted by the English Revolution of 1688, became a standard for European and American liberals in the eighteenth century (see: Maurice Duverger, *Introduction à la Politique*, Paris: Gallimard, 1964). The first group to use the "liberal" label in a political context was the Spanish political party of the "Liberales," which persistently fought for the implementation of the 1812 Constitution, and, in 1820, it overthrew the Spanish monarchy as part of the "Trienio Liberal." Arguably, the most important bourgeois revolution in the modern era is the French Revolution of 1789, whose major motto was "Liberty, Equality, Fraternity." However, the elite of the bourgeois class conceived capitalism as the embodiment of human freedom in the domain of economics, and, for this reason, after the displacement of feudalism by capitalism, the liberty and the rights of the human individual were gradually largely displaced by and subordinated to the liberty and the rights of the capital itself and the capitalist elite. Moreover, the rationalism of traditional liberalism and the original bourgeois class was gradually substituted and dominated by the selfish expediencies and passions of the capitalists, transforming the rationalist underpinnings and principles of classical political economy into contradictory and empirically insignificant assertions.

• *The ideology of socialism:* By the middle of the nineteenth century, the European peoples realized that capitalism had displaced feudalism, but, instead of ushering in liberty, equality, and fraternity among the people, capitalism tends to replace the authoritarian and exploitative relationship between the feudal lords and the serfs with a new authoritarian and exploitative relationship, namely, that between the capitalist class and the proletariat (working-class). Therefore, socialism emerged as a criticism of and a revolt against capitalism, just as the bourgeois ideology had previously emerged as a criticism of and a revolt against feudalism. In fact, the term "socialism" first appeared in 1832 in *Le Globe,* a liberal French newspaper of the French philosopher and political economist Pierre Leroux, and, by the 1840s, socialism had already become the object of rigorous social-scientific analysis by the German economist and sociologist Lorenz von Stein. Moreover, the English socialist intellectual and activist Thomas Hodgskin (1787-1869) articulated a thorough critical analysis of capitalism and of the labor class under capitalism, and his writings exerted a significant influence on subsequent generations of socialists, including Karl Marx. In particular, from the perspective of Thomas Hodgskin, socialism signifies an attempt to create a rational and fair market, in the context of which production and exchange are based on the labor theory of value (freed from exploitative institutions) as part of natural right, which endows moral consciousness, the freedom of the individual, social justice, and social autonomy with ontological underpinnings (in accordance with Thomas Hodgskin's deism). In addition, the

Russian-Soviet philosopher and scientist Alexander Bogdanov, one of the acknowledged founders of the science of planning and organizational theory, has argued that socialism is meaningless without a "universal organizational science" capable of combining and coordinating all the individual disciplines.

• *The ideology of nationalism:* The ideology of nationalism is a product of the synthesis between liberalism and romanticism. Rationalism gives primacy to thought vales (which are characterized by intellectual abstraction and universalism) over life values (which are characterized by sensationalism and particularity). Hence, rationalism underpins cosmopolitanism. By contrast, romanticism, giving primacy to life values over thought values, underpins communitarianism. The ideology of nationalism is inextricably linked to Hegel's communitarianism. Opposing Kant, who is the paradigmatic representative of critical rationalism, Hegel maintains that the human individual exists truly as a conscious being only within the nation, and one can ascend to the universal spirit only if and to the extent that one's spiritual freedom is self-abolished and absorbed by the community. Hence, according to Hegel, the individuality of the citizen presupposes the individuality of the state. Furthermore, Hegel's account of international politics is set out in sections 321–340 of the *Philosophy of Right*. According to Hegel, the state is absolutely sovereign, that is, there can be no higher authority than the state.

• *The ideology of the "loyalists," conservatism, and fascism:* The ideology of the "loyalists," the "loyal people" (whether "loyalism" refers to a Sovereign or the established constitution), is strongly related to political conservatism and fascism. A constituent element of the ideology of the "loyalists" is the substitution of politics by moral attitudes. The conservative political attitude is characterized by fear of reversals and revolts, by faith in the measured, in harmony, in unity, in the eternal, in the immutable, in the absolute, in the opposition of soul to matter, but it is mainly characterized by the belief that the ills of society are the faults of the individuals themselves, whose improvement is the only remedy for the progress of society (thus ignoring or silencing the flaws of the social system itself). In the twentieth century, in the Western capitalist camp, the rise of the fear of the "communist threat" led to the fusion of populism and conservatism within the ideology of "loyalism," thus producing two new ideological currents: fascism and neoconservatism.

- *The ideology of the "nation-minded people":* In the era of globalization, particularly, from the 1960s onwards, the ideology of the "nation-minded people" expresses a synthesis between the ideology of the bourgeois-liberals and the ideology of the "loyalists," and, in particular, this synthesis leads to the coexistence of the institution of the nation-state with the globalization of political economy. Whereas traditional nationalism is contrary to globalization, the ideology of the "nation-minded people" adapts traditional nationalism to the needs of globalization, altering traditional nationalism so that the preservation of traditional national ideas and institutions is combined with acquiescence to globalized capitalism.

The Autonomous Order of the Modern and Perfecting Rite of Symbolic Masonry promotes a specific ideology, which I have called "critical rational socialism." In the context of my theory of critical rational socialism, the head of government (namely, the "supreme leader" of a socialist polity) and the Central Economic Planning Authority (CEPA) represent an updated, modern version of Plato's political vision. The vertical and technocratic hierarchical system that I propose stands in stark contrast to libertarian socialism, libertarian communism, and postmodern leftism, but it should not be confused with other historical models, such as those of the tyrant, the dictator, the monarch, and similar others. The CEPA is analogous with the government of philosophers delineated by Plato in the *Republic*, and, of course, it is in agreement with Marx's, Engels's, and the Soviet cyberneticians' positions on and conceptions of scientific socialism.

Chapter 2

Initiatory Systems

"Initiation" means the ability to see when your eyes are shut, specifically, it means the ability to see beyond the phenomena of the sensible world. The presence of any being of the sensible world in human consciousness is determined by the significance that human consciousness assigns to it. Thus, the ability to see beyond sensible phenomena means that one is able to see the spiritual reality (that is, the system of meanings and values) in which the objects of one's consciousness are embedded.

Tau Dr. Allen Bar Kohenim Greenfield, one of the most important contemporary authorities on occultism in general and the Ancient and Primitive Rite of Memphis-Misraim in particular, has succinctly explained the significance of "ritual initiations," as practiced, for instance, by Freemasons, as follows: firstly, an initiatory ritual is the product of its composer, who seeks to get the candidate from a point A to a point B according to a specific process; and secondly, an initiatory ritual is a product of action, specifically, of the act of initiation by a trained initiate, charged with the duty of conducting the candidate through a ceremony in such a way that a receptive candidate will experience the intended inner alteration and personal growth (see: http://tallengreenfield.com/index.html).[1]

Genuine and worthy esoteric schools lead their members to a state of joy. In fact, the value of an esoteric school and the qualities of one's initiatory itinerary can be tested by the extent to which they provide joy. It is important to understand the difference between "pleasure" and "joy." Pleasure is a positive sentiment that is produced by external stimuli, in the sense that we feel pleasure only as long as an external source of pleasure continues to provide us with its positive sensuous feedback; for instance,

---

[1] See also: Allen H. Greenfield, *The Compleat Rite of Memphis*, second edition, CreateSpace Independent Publishing Platform, 2014.

nice tastes, nice scents, nice company, pleasant gatherings, good news, material rewards, sexual satisfaction, etc. However, as soon as an external source of pleasure ceases to provide us with its positive sensuous feedback, we cease to feel pleasure. By contrast, joy is an emotional state that comes from the inside, specifically, from our own spirituality, and it is independent of external stimuli. Thus, a person who has achieved a high level of spiritual development may continue feeling joy, which stems exactly from his/her spiritual development, even when he/she experiences negative, namely, unpleasant, external stimuli, such as deterioration in his/her financial or health condition, unjust treatment, loneliness, etc. Thus, as the apostle Paul writes in his epistle to the Hebrews, Jesus endured the cross for the joy set before him, and, in John's Gospel, we read that Jesus Christ said to his disciples that he made them partakers of his Logos so that his joy may be with them.

On the other hand, today, many esoteric schools, either because they are spiritually disoriented or because they are focused on the principle of pleasure, as opposed to the principle of joy, cannot produce spiritually free and esoterically joyful persons, but they produce individuals who are outer-directed and addicted to external stimuli. Thus, for instance, many contemporary Freemasonic institutions try to recruit new members and keep their old ones in good standing by claiming and insinuating that their participation in Freemasonry will primarily be a source of pleasant stimuli, that is, they emphasize the exoteric aspects of Masonic interactions combined with or rather cloaked with a few elementary moralistic premises, even though the essence of Freemasonry consists of esoteric experiences and esoteric labors. For instance, in the context of the Emulation Ritual, which is the most widely practiced English Masonic ritual, we learn that Freemasonry "teaches moral lessons and self-knowledge through participation in a progression of allegorical plays, learnt by heart and performed within the Lodge." And as the traditional lessons and insights of the degree-system of Freemasonry envelop, guide, and guard you, you gain new perspectives and awarenesses of yourself, your fellow-humans, and your universe. However, even though the majority of Lodge meetings should be held in order to go on a journey of learning and, thus, to engage in philosophical, theological, scientific, and socio-political debate, discourse, and exposition, the truth is that most contemporary so-called regular Masonic Lodges meet almost exclusively in order to conduct degree ceremonies, collect alms and fees, and engage in exoteric, if not profane, social interactions. As a matter of fact, this is one of the main reasons why I have created a distinct and independent Masonic Order, namely, in order to be able to avail ourselves of esoteric Freemasonry and Freemasonic esotericism.

2.1 Orphism and Pythagoreanism

The beginnings of esotericism can be traced back to Orphism, the greatest mystery cult of sixth-century B.C. Greece. This period was important not only for the birth of philosophy, but, above all, for religious history, because it was this century that saw the emergence of Confucius and Lao-Tse in China, the Buddha in India, Zoroaster in Iran, and Pythagoras among the Greeks.

As the distinguished scholar and esotericist Giuliano Di Bernardo has pointed out, "the sixth century B.C. in Greece was an era of profound social transformations, coming between the collapse of the ancient monarchies described in the poems of Homer and the rise of the democratic states, of which Athens is the most striking example," and, in this historical context, "Orphism represented a yearning for liberation from the oppression of the oligarchic regimes of those troubled times, a sacred refuge for the chosen spirits, and a means for reaching towards moral perfection within a religious cosmogony."[2]

"Awaken the memory of the solemn *telete* [=ceremonies] in the mystai [=initiates]" is the prayer of initiates in the Orphic hymn to Mnemosyne, the goddess of Memory, referring to an effect of different order.[3] A more specific function is given to "memory" by the theory of "transmigration of souls." The participation in mystery festivals was a life-transforming experience, specifically, a *pathos* in the soul of the candidate, since it was cultivating an attitude of introspection. Aristotle, in the rediscovered fragment 15 of his treatise *On Philosophy*, maintains that, at the final stage of the ancient Greek initiatory rites, there should be no more "learning" (*mathein*) but "experiencing" (*pathein*) and a change in the stage of mind (*diatethenai*), and, for this reason, initiatory rites push conceptual knowledge into the background in favor of mystical iconic visions.[4]

2   The aforementioned statements by Professor and Masonic Grand Master Giuliano Di Bernardo are included in his essay *Freemasonry: A Philosophical Investigation*, which he personally communicated with me on 14 November 2018.
3   *Orph. Hymn.* 77:9.
4   See: W. D. Ross, *Aristotelis Fragmenta Selecta*, Oxford: Clarendon, 1955.

The central god of Orphism was Dionysus, the youngest Olympian god, who, like Orpheus, was from Thrace and is well known for his suffering and his unjust death. The gods of Olympus, who had glorified the old warrior aristocracy extolled by Homer and represented a more extroverted attitude, increasingly lost their importance in favor of a more esoteric approach to religion and in favor of more introverted attitudes.

Depending on the corresponding cult, the Thraco-Phrygian god Dionysus emerged as a surrogate for Attis, who was the consort of Cybele (an Anatolian mother goddess) in Phrygian and Greek mythology, or Adonis, who was the mortal lover of the goddess Aphrodite in Greek mythology. As Giuliano Di Bernardo has pointedly observed, "the importance of the cult of Dionysus was not only due to its reference to the principles of fertility and agriculture, but also to its element of drama, in the person of the god himself."[5] Moreover, it is worth pointing out that Plato, in the dialogue Phaedrus, has Dionysus presiding over "telestic madness," and he specifies that these are rituals performed for therapeutic purposes. "Teletai [=ceremonies] and purifications" are performed by people masking as Nymphs, Panes, Silens, and Satyrs, as Plato writes in his Laws.[6]

Whereas the Apollonian religious attitude is focused on the "here and now," the Dionysian religious attitude refers to an opportunized tomorrow, or, in other words, to a salvational and accessible hereafter. Moreover, as early as in Euripides's *Bacchae* (465-474, 232-238), a charismatic itinerant – alias Dionysus – appears on stage as a stranger from Lydia who offers his *teletai* (that is, his rituals) and performs miracles, claiming to have received his *orgia* (that is, his holy practices) in direct revelation form his god.

Orphism is based on the mysteries of Dionysus. There is a rich variety of Bacchic mythology, but the ancient Greek mysteries were inspired and underpinned by only one myth about Dionysus: the story of Chthonian Dionysus born from Persephone (the venerable majestic princess of the underworld) and slaughtered, specifically, dismembered, by the Titans, the ancestors of humanity. From the perspective of depth psychology, Dionysus, as the god of drama, and especially the murder of Dionysus (deicide) can serve as symbols in remembering, specifically, reuniting, our torn apart body and psyche.

---

5   Giuliano Di Bernardo, *Freemasonry: A Philosophical Investigation,* unpublished essay personally communicated to me by its author, 14 November 2018.
6   See: Louis Bouyer, "Mystique: Essai sur l'histoire d'un mot," Supplément de *La Vie spirituelle,* 15 Mai 1949, pp. 3-23

According to the ancient Greek mysteries, atonement could be attained in two ways: rebirth into other bodies or ritual purification. The highest aspiration for Orphics was to break the "circle of generations," which turned inexorably like a wheel, namely, the wheel of destiny, in order finally to return to the originating cause. The second method was to live a pure life of asceticism and purification through ritual ceremonies, since it was believed that the period of atonement could be reduced by choosing a mode of life inspired by the highest moral values and by practicing the proper rituals.

In the ancient Greco-Roman world, there were two forms of religion: "public" religion, which consisted in worship of Olympian deities, and the "mystery" cults. According to Giuliano Di Bernardo, "the existence of a mystery religion was the clearest possible sign that the official religion was incapable of interpreting the need for an authentic religious sense," and "it is to a mystery religion – namely, Orphism – that we attribute a decisive influence on the growing philosophy movement."[7] This was primarily due to the fact that Orphism signals a dramatic shift away from the reality of the world itself (namely, the subject-matter of the so-called natural philosophy) to the reality of the human consciousness and seeks to liberate the latter from necessities that appear to be derived from the first and, ultimately, to revisit and interpret the reality of the world from a human perspective. Thus, the "theology" of the Orphic cult is intimately related to anthropology. The Orphic cult gave rise to a primitive form of philosophical anthropology, since it developed a dualistic conception of the human being, where the human soul was equivalent with the divine element, and the body was the place (or, rather, the "prison") of the soul's atonement. A variant of the Orphics' dualistic conception of the human being and the attempt to transcend dualism and achieve internal (psychological) and external (cosmic) harmony underpin the works of Pythagoras, Heraclitus, Socrates, Plato, and all the philosophers who have based their own thought on theirs.

With Orphism and the philosophies of Pythagoras and Plato, the human mind was "discovered" as something different from the surrounding body of nature and capable of discerning similarities in a multiplicity of events. Hence, Plato, in the *Republic*, argues that "the dialectical mind" is *synoptikos*, that is, it takes a "synoptic view" of scattered objects, in the

---

7   Giuliano Di Bernardo, *Freemasonry (ibid). Moreover, see: Giuliano Di Bernardo, Freemasonry and Its Image of Man: A Philosophical Investigation,* Tunbridge Wells (England): Freestone, 1989.

sense that it seeks to understand them through and within the unity of the corresponding idea, which is their "logos," that is, their efficient and final cause, their ultimate meaning. Furthermore, the Greeks' confidence in the essential reasonableness of nature and the associated feeling that, beneath the perplexing heterogeneity and ceaseless flux of events, the human mind can find elements of harmony and beauty underpin the Pythagorean School, another offshoot of Orphism. The Pythagorean School was founded by Pythagoras in Croton, Magna Graecia, in around 530 B.C.

In the Pythagorean School, which was a philosophical, religious, and scientific fraternity, the disciples were divided into the "acousmatics" ("listeners"), who followed the lesson in silence and devoted themselves to its interpretation, and the "mathematicians" ("learners"), who were permitted to converse with the teacher and were taught the deeper aspects of scientific knowledge. Pythagoras's fundamental beliefs are the following: (i) Nature and, in general, the universe have an underlying mathematical structure. (ii) The ultimate purpose of philosophy is spiritual purification. (iii) The pure soul can rise to experience the union with the deity. (iv) Certain symbols, including mathematical ones, have a mystical significance. (v) All those who were initiated into Pythagoras's Order should observe strict loyalty and secrecy.

The geometric theorem that bears Pythagoras's name[8] differs from similar geometric perceptions and measurements that had been achieved by Babylonians and Egyptians because Pythagoras's and, generally, ancient Greek scientists' thought is characterized by a persistent search for universals, whereas the Babylonian and the Egyptian mathematicians were not only ignorant of Plato's "synoptic" method, but they also lacked Aristotle's and the Greek mathematicians' tendency towards the isolation and abstraction of certain samenesses from their concomitants. Therefore, the Babylonians' and the Egyptians' mathematical achievements lack the hypothetico-deductive structure of the Greek mathematics. Furthermore, the Pythagorean School had esoteric and initiatory foundations, just like Orphism.

Orpheus and Pythagoras, who were luminous expressions of philosophy in its infancy, gave rise to a secret tradition that has played a very important role in the history of esotericism. In the context of the Orphic tradition, rhythm and music gave rise to a form of ecstasy that takes on the

---

8   The Pythagorean Theorem, states that, in every right-angled triangle, the square of the hypotenuse is equal to the sum of the squares of the other two sides.

meaning of a surrogate for death and transcends the senses, thus offering entry to a transcendent world that lies beyond the grave. In fact, Euripides breaks down the orgiastic process into three distinct stages in his character "Hercules the Madman."[9] Both Orphism and Pythagoreanism, each in its own way, made use of certain elements of the aforementioned psychosocial and religious disposition (namely, the journey towards a transcendent, eternal world), and, by relying on that disposition, they were able to articulate an explanation of the cosmos and of the humankind with greater ease and to endow the existence of the cosmos and of the humankind with a transcendent meaning.

2.2 Gnosticism

What is a Gnostic? This is a loaded question. To try to answer it would be to invoke the wrath of Gnostics whose views are not included in the reply. There is no one answer, because there are different schools of Gnosticism, and this system of spirituality speaks to different people in different ways, as arguably it should. As the Gnostic researcher and podcaster Miguel Conner pointedly argued in the Introduction to his book *Voices of Gnosticism* (Dublin: Bardic Press, 2010), "Gnostics never possessed a unified monolithic theology. They had an underlying structure of themes, but these were just a bedrock to build cities of theosophical inquiry without much legalistic zoning." One can find Gnostics who have reconciled Gnosticism with Christianity, Buddhism, Islam, Judaism, etc. Already in the second century A.D., there were different schools of Gnosticism (see for instance: Aldo Magris, "Gnosticism: Gnosticism from Its Origins to the Middle Ages," in *Encyclopedia of Religion*, second edition, edited by Lindsay Jones, Detroit: Macmillan, 2005). However, following Miguel Conner's research legacy, I believe that the question deserves more respect than the usual generic answer according to which Gnosticism, being derived from the Greek word "gnosis" (knowledge), refers to a specialized knowledge of the way things really are and the means by which humans can extricate themselves from their captivity to a fallen material world.

Speaking from a rigidly doctrinal and formalistic perspective does not do much for the elucidation of Gnosticism either, because it contradicts

---

9   See: F. Ferrini, "Tragodia e patologia: Lessico ippocratico in Euripide," *Quaderni Urbinati di Cultura Classica*, vol. 29, 1978, pp. 49-62; Jennifer C. Kosak, *Heroic Measures: Hippocratic Medicine in the Making of Euripidean Tragedy*, Leiden: Brill, 2004.

and undermines some of the spiritually most fruitful attributes of Gnosticism, namely the following: (i) the indeterminacy of meaning (the signified), which is an attribute not only of the most inspiring Gnostic texts but also of the most inspiring creations of the human spirit in general, thus underpinning their allure independently of space-time constraints; (ii) the use of a language that helps people to communicate with each other regarding that which transcends words and concepts by using symbols and allegories; (iii) the development of a poetic, as opposed to a technocratic, approach to the transcendent; and (iv) the endorsement of an attitude towards religion whose purpose is the spiritualization of the material world rather than the formalization of spirituality. The four aforementioned attributes of Gnosticism are, in my opinion, necessary components of every spiritually fruitful approach to Gnosticism, because, in this way, Gnosticism remains spiritually relevant and useful in different segments of historical space-time and to different cultural communities. Therefore, I construe and propose Gnosticism as a set of questions and spiritual quests and as a peculiar way of posing questions and inspiring spiritual quests rather than as a set of particular answers and formalistic cultural recipes.

Consciousness is not merely a framework within which the accumulation of experiences takes place, but it is a living and structured presence that has all the attributes of a being – namely, substance, structure, temporal and spatial activity – and it is continuously restructured, determining the laws of its activity, its intentionality and its integration in the world. Thus, consciousness is the fullest expression of the reality of the human being.

The philosophy of existence, known also as "existentialism," highlights the distinction between the essence of being and the presence of being. The philosophy of existence has its roots in the works of Augustine of Hippo and Blaise Pascal, but its founders were Søren A. Kierkegaard, Martin Heidegger, Karl Jaspers, Jean-Paul Sartre, and Hans Jonas (see for instance: Steven Earnshaw, *Existentialism: A Guide for the Perplexed*, London: Continuum, 2006; Thomas Flynn, *Existentialism: A Very Short Introduction*, Oxford: Oxford University Press, 2006; Robert Solomon, ed., *Existentialism*, New York: Random House, 1974). Whereas Aristotle's philosophy assigns primary significance to the essence of things (namely, to the attribute or set of attributes that makes an object what it fundamentally is, and which an object has by necessity, and without which it loses its identity), the philosophers of existence are primarily concerned with the presence of being, namely, with its existence. In other words, existentialists are primarily concerned with the very fact that a being exists and is present, in one way or another (ether in front of someone or independently of one's consciousness), and/or with the manner in which one can identify a being. Thus, from the perspective of existentialism, ontology is centered on the following two issues: (i) the fact that one is conscious of that which exists outside oneself and (ii) the fact that one is conscious of one's own existence. In particular, J.-P. Sartre argued that the objects of one's consciousness (namely, one's conscious contents and everything that one is aware of) exist not only "in themselves" but also "for oneself," and the same holds for one's own existence, too (see: Thomas Busch, *The Power of Consciousness and the Force of Circumstances in Sartre's Philosophy*, Bloomington: Indiana University Press, 1990).

The argument that the concepts of "essence" and "presence" should not be identified with each other follows logically from the fact that essence can be conceived as independent of its reality. For instance, I accept that Chimera is an imaginary creature that is not real in the external animal kingdom, but I can define Chimera by specifying its qualities (namely, its essence): a monstrous fire-breathing female creature born by Typhon and Echidna, and composed of the parts of multiple animals: upon the body of a lioness with a tail that ended in a snake's head, the head of a goat arose on her back at the center of her spine. By thus defining Chimera, I specify its essence, but I do not argue for its existence. In the context of human consciousness, "essence" and "presence" are not identical to each other.

At the level of the divine Being, essence is identified with presence as, for instance, we read in the Bible, where one of God's names is "I am that I am" (Exodus, 3:14), but, at the level of consciousness, existence is prior to essence, not so much in the sense of chronological order but of significance. In other words, from the perspective of existentialism, consciousness assigns primary significance to the emergence of existence out of non-existence, and, thus, ontology reduces to a "genealogy" of existence. From the aforementioned perspective, the first priority of the philosophers of existence consists in the following dual task: firstly, they have to explain the manner in which human existence and human knowledge progress from one level of being and one level of knowledge to another; secondly, they have to explain the manner in which consciousness evolves gradually by confronting its own antinomies, thus progressing from an immediate and unformed state to a condition of inner unity and integral self-experience. In particular, Karl Jaspers, ascribed central status to "limit situations" (*Grenzsituationen*), which are moments, usually accompanied by experiences of dread, guilt or acute anxiety, in which the human mind confronts the restrictions and pathological narrowness of its existing forms, and allows itself to abandon the security of its limitedness and so to enter a new realm of self-consciousness (see: Paul A. Schilpp, ed., *The Philosophy of Karl Jaspers*, New York: Tudor Publishing Company, 1957). Additionally, Jaspers developed a theory of the "unconditioned" (*das Unbedingte*), arguing that human limitations are neither absolute nor fixed, and, in general, human life is basically about growing and outgrowing our old, immature and less perfect ways.

The prominent existentialist philosopher and Gnostic researcher Hans Jonas, who taught philosophy at the New School for Social Research in New York City from 1955 to 1976, articulated an existentialist interpretation of Gnosticism by arguing that Gnosticism can be construed as an existential methodology that provides humanity with a peculiar way of understanding:

- the meaning of Being (emphasizing personal relationship and experience),

- the situation of humanity,

- the structure and the importance of selfhood, and

- the struggle for the salvation (perfection) of selfhood and for the protection of selfhood from the powers of alienation that impinge on humanity.

Hence, Jonas maintains that the fundamental questions that guided and inspired the Gnostics are summarized by the following fragment ascribed to Theodotos, a proponent of the Valentinian school of Gnosticism: "*what makes us free is the knowledge [gnosis] of who we were, what we have become; where we were, wherein we have been thrown; whereto we speed, wherefrom we are redeemed; what is birth and what rebirth*" (Hans Jonas, *The Gnostic Religion: The Message of the Alien God and the Beginnings of Christianity*, third edition, Boston: Beacon Press, 2001, p. 334).

From the aforementioned perspective, gnosis, namely, the peculiar kind of knowledge pursued by the Gnostics, can be interpreted as the mystical, psychically purifying and existentially liberating kind of knowledge pursued by the Ancient Mysteries, Plato (*Republic*, 560e, 580d; *Phaedo*, 65e-66a, 67e, 74a-c, 114c; *Cratylus*, 396c, 405a-b), Hermeticism, the various "schools" of the Kabbalah, Alchemy, and the various Christian mystics (including the Rosicrucians and the Byzantine hesychasts). In particular, the aforementioned "Jonasian" approach to Gnosticism implies that, by fusing existentialism and Gnosticism, the Gnostics' critique of the world, far from being a spiritually sterile and psychologically flawed world-negating attitude, implies a process of "demundanization" (*Entweltlichung*), in the context of which the human being renounces "worldliness" (rather than the "world" itself) and follows an actively emancipatory spiritual journey. By using Jonas's existentialism as an interpretive framework in order to understand the relationship between the "Gnostic mind" and the external world, we realize that the "Gnostic mind" does not (necessarily) renounce the world itself, but it definitely strives, firstly, to transcend the level of consciousness that is determined by the logic of the established world order and, secondly, to create better existential conditions under which one will affirm one's own existence. This is the meaning of renouncing "worldliness" rather than the "world" itself. By renouncing worldliness, the Gnostic reinforces one's self-directedness vis-à-vis the world and, particularly, wrestles "against the authorities, against the powers, against the world-ruling forces of the darkness of this Aeon, against the spiritual forces of evil in the heavenly realms" (Ephesians 6:12; I translate from the original ancient Greek text). Therefore, by fusing the philosophy of existence, Gnostic mysticism, and the Gnostics' renouncing of worldliness, we come up with a philosophy of existential emancipation and continuous metaphysical revolt, since the human being's innermost self, one's spirit (namely, that part of our being which transcends pure biology), takes pride in a transcendent, supramundane origin, namely, in "this region beyond the skies," which is "the abode of the reality with which true knowledge is concerned, a reality without color or shape, intangible," as Plato put it in his *Phaedrus* (247c-e).

As a result, Gnosticism's attitude towards the world should not be considered exclusively rejectionist, since, from the perspective of existential Gnosticism, Gnosticism's negative attitude towards the world expresses a psychically grown up person's attempt to proclaim and manifest one's individuation (vis-à-vis the world order) and impose one's intentionality on the world (hence, create an autonomous civilization), and it is matched and underpinned by a vision of the human being as a god-in-the-making (a potential deity). The archaic type of psyche, in general, and those interpretations of Gnosticism that assign a passive role to the human psyche (under the influence of archaic and/or oriental mentalities), in particular, aim to impose an order on the movements of the human psyche by harmonizing the human psyche with the universal rhythm or the universal order, and, therefore, they tend to privilege negative concepts, such as ancient Greeks' fear of hubris and certain ancient Gnostics' sense of alienation and dependence on a cosmic dialectic. On the other hand, a psyche that has achieved the goal of individuation (and, hence, is grown up), in general, and the aforementioned existentialist approach to Gnosticism, which assigns an active role to the human psyche, in particular, aim to impose an order on the movements of the human psyche through humanity's inner, mystical communion with the ultimate source of the significance of the beings and things that exist in the world, thus internalizing the deity instead of being externally determined by and/or harmonized with the logic of a given world order. The aforementioned existentialist approach to Gnosticism is striving for humanity's authentic mode of being and freedom, and it expresses humanity's intention to restructure the reality of the world according to the intentionality of human consciousness, whenever humanity experiences the world as a place of isolation and exile. Hence, I maintain that the Gnostic struggle can be considered in this sense to be a strategy of continuous metaphysical revolt.

The ingenious and highly literally cultivated occultist Aleister Crowley put it succinctly and aptly in his essay *The Soldier and the Hunchback: ! And ?* (Liber CLVIII, 1909): "*My message is then twofold; to the greasy 'bourgeois' I preach discontent; I shock him, I stagger him, I cut away earth from under his feet, I turn him upside down, I give him hashish and make him run amok, I twitch his buttocks with the red-hot tongs of my Sadistic fancy— until he feels uncomfortable. But to the man who is already as uneasy as St. Lawrence on his silver grill, who feels the spirit stir in him, even as a woman feels, and sickens at, the first leap of the babe in her womb, to him I bring the splendid vision, the perfume and the glory, the Knowledge and Conversation of the Holy Guardian Angel. And to whosoever hath attained that height will I put a further Question, announce a further Glory.*"

By construing Gnosticism as a strategy of continuous metaphysical revolt, and by endorsing a vision of the human being as a potential god according to the aforementioned existentialist approach to Gnosticism, we realize and highlight the submissiveness of history to the intentionality of human consciousness. This rationale lies in the philosophy of history that is part of my theory of rational dynamicity (delineated in Chapter 1).

The traditional Gnostic texts are very rich in symbolism, allegorical narratives, and poetry. In the context of Gnostic literature, the term "Archon" (which is a Greek word literally meaning "ruler") refers to demonic rulers of the material world, usually considered to be demonic entities subordinate to the embodiment of evil. For instance, in Manichaeism, the Archons are the rulers of a realm within the "Kingdom of Darkness" who together make up the Prince of Darkness. However, according to the second-century A.D. Gnostic master Basilides, there existed a "Great Archon" called Abraxas, who presided over 365 Archons. Moreover, in the Apocryphon of John (a second-century A.D. Sethian Gnostic Christian text of secret teachings), we read the following: *Now the Archon [ruler], who is weak, has three names. The first name is Yaldabaoth [the "Lion-faced," the deity of control], the second is Saklas [the "Fool," the deity of ignorance and intellectual darkness], and the third is Samael [the "Venom of God," the deity of seduction and destruction]. And he is impious in his arrogance, which is in him. For he said, 'I am God, and there is no other God beside me,' for he is ignorant of his strength, the place from which he had come.*

From the perspective of existential Gnosticism, which I delineate and propose in this essay, the concept of "Archon" or "Archontic force/entity" refers to any historical, psychological, and/or spiritual force/entity that has the following three goals: firstly, to deprive the human being of the awareness of humanity's divine potential and to make humans think of God as a judgmental and despotic spiritual overlord and not as the Archetype of the Human Being; secondly, to prevent humanity from manifesting its free will and from acting according to the intentionality of one's enlightened consciousness; and, thirdly, to narrow and manipulate humanity's intellectual and, generally, existential horizons by subjugating humans to existential conditions and ways of thinking that are deemed objectively necessary and rational whereas, in essence, they are institutions created by the Archons themselves. Hence, as we read in Matthew 23:13, the Archontic forces (such as "the teachers of the law and

Pharisees") "shut the kingdom of heaven in men's faces," and, because the Archons themselves do not enter the realm of pure Gnosis (namely, the divine mode of being), they do not permit others to enter when they try.

Many people tend to think that several ideas and pursuits, such as freedom, equality, justice, and truth, are somehow self-evident, and that, in every historical segment of space-time, the human being promoted and investigated them. This is a historical illusion. For the most part, the hitherto known human societies existed under conditions where humans accepted, without question, those ideas, values, ruling norms, and ways of life which the institutionalized tradition of the corresponding society had imposed on them and had raised them with. However, throughout history, there has been a special, illumined minority of people who raise the aforementioned subject-matters and ideas, create movements for the amelioration and spiritual evolution of humanity by means of conquering error and aiding humans in their efforts of attaining the power of knowing the truth, and even cause social and political revolutions. This illumined minority consists of highly initiated mystics, philosophers, scientists, artists, social scholars, and political revolutionaries. Moreover, there have been a few societies and historical moments in which the aforementioned subject-matters and ideas were raised by many people and in which there emerged a social/political movement involving almost the entire population, at least potentially, and people started massively to question the traditional views of the world, the traditional ideas concerning what is worthwhile and what is not, what is fair and what is not, and to reflect on key philosophical and political questions such as the following: "How should society be instituted?", "What is justice?," "How are we to think?," "What is good life?," "What is truth?," "What is one's real interest?," etc. For instance, this occurred in ancient Greek societies from the eighth century B.C. until the end of the fifth century B.C. and in several Western European societies after the end of the Middle Ages.

In general, every society institutes itself, that is, it creates its own institutions on the basis of a system of fundamental significations that orientate and guide the values and the activity of the people in a society. This system of fundamental significations is the constitutive myth, that is, the spiritual core, of the corresponding society. Such fundamental significations can be neither rationally confirmed nor rationally refuted. Hence, they belong to the sphere of the myth. For instance, the existence of Jehovah or the Christian God cannot be rationally proven, and, for similar reasons, any attempt to rationally refute His existence is cognitively insignificant. Furthermore, the capitalist society sets as its major fundamental signification the accumulation of capital and the "homo economicus" (a model for human behavior characterized by selfishness and the unlimited expansion of a rationalized domination over nature and over humans themselves), and it presents this as a rational pursuit, whereas this pursuit, which is a key underpinning of the capitalist society, is essentially non-rational and originates from the realm of mythology, since it reflects a particular type of human being (a particular "ideal"). Why should rationality consist in the capitalists' own idea of an endless expansion of domination, and what does domination really mean? Should the idea of domination also refer to domination over passions and illusions, or should it only refer to one's domination over external conditions and other humans? From a strictly logical perspective, the capitalists' own idea of an endless expansion of domination is as non-rational as the idea of Jehovah or the Christian God. In general, the most important issues, ultimately, depend on myth rather than logic. This is the reason why, ultimately, the most important truths do not carry unshakable certainties around with them, but they are burning, since they require (and emerge from) existentially crucial decisions by human consciousness.

According to existential Gnosticism and the strategy of continuous metaphysical revolt, which I delineate and propose in this essay as a general way of thinking about spirituality and politology (prior to and independently of committing oneself to a particular religious, intellectual, and/or political group), our existential conditions are not primarily determined by things themselves or by imperishable necessities, but they are primarily determined by the way in which we give meaning to things and to our existence itself and by the freedom of the spirit. In order to avoid being trapped in an Archontic system, we must have a vigilant mind capable of analyzing and evaluating the fundamental significations on which every grand narrative and, in general, every argument are based, and we must be fully aware of the source of the significance of the beings and things that exist in the world.

A really free and creative person is aware that the most important decision in one's life is not one's rationalized adaptation to an established system, but the conscious choice of a vital myth, namely, of a system of fundamental significations that will make one's life meaningful and will guide one's conduct and historical action. In other words, the most important decision in one's life is the development of a conscious personal relationship with God, since, by the term "God," I mean the positive void, the transcendent Source, from which the significance of the beings and things derive. The way in which one perceives God and one's relationship with God determines one's world-conception, self-conception, and way of life. In John 10:34, we read that humans are potentially gods, but the Archons' power is determined by the extent to which they convince people to treat Archons as self-subsistent real "gods," or as natural/historical necessities, and to forget that the human being is a potential god. An Archon (or a group of Archons) creates a system and tries to convince the people that live in the given Archontic system that it is an imperishable necessity dictated by the intrinsic logic of nature and/or history, whereas, in reality, it is a creation of a particular Archon (or of a particular group of Archons). Hence, my conception of continuous metaphysical revolt consists in the willingness and the ability to revolt against any force that aims to deprive humans of their divine potential, to make them oblivious of their free will, creativity, and divine potential, and to subjugate them to the logic of a supposedly all-powerful, redoubtable material system.

2.3 Kabbalah

First of all, we must clarify that the Kabbalah has two meanings. Firstly, it refers to the esoteric interpretation of orthodox rabbinic Judaism. In Hebrew, "Kabbalah" means "acception," and, in a sense, it means "tradition," too. Secondly, the term "Kabbalah" stands for an ecumenical esoteric system of correspondences and symbols (this type of Kabbalah, in particular, is sometimes spelled "Qabalah"). The Kabbalah uses notions and symbols of the original Jewish Kabbalistic tradition in order to give rise to a new, anthropocentric and esoteric system of humanity's progress, which plays a protagonist role in the Western esoteric tradition. Therefore, in the context of Western esotericism, the Kabbalah constitutes an esoteric methodology that transcends the Jewish and any other religion.

The primary Kabbalistic treatises are the *Wisdom of Solomon*, the *Zohar* (or *Book of Light*), and the *Sefer Yetsira* (or *Book of the Creation*). The treatise Wisdom of Solomon is said to have been written in Hellenistic Alexandria, and it is attributed to Philo of Alexandria (ca. 25 B.C.-ca. 50

A.D.), a Hellenistic Jewish philosopher, whose purpose was to harmonize Greek philosophy with Jewish spirituality. Philo's allegorical and symbolic treatises and his concept of the Logos as God's creative principle were important for several Christian Church fathers, and they influenced early Christology. The *Zohar* was written by Simeon bar Yochai and first printed in Mantua in 1558. The author of the *Sefer Yetsira* is unknown, and scholars place its origin at sometime between 100 B.C. and 800 A.D., but it was originally published in Provence, in the thirteenth century A.D., by Rabbi Isaac ben Abraham.

The Kabbalistic symbol that is called the "Tree of Life" is frequently mentioned in the Jewish religious texts, including the Torah. This symbolic tree contains ten fruits called the "Sefirot" (emanations; singular form: "Sefira"), and they are connected together by twenty two paths corresponding to the Hebrew letters, alchemical, and astrological principles. The Sefirot have been referred to as "the ten faces of God," and, since, according to the Bible, humans were created in the image of God, the Tree of Life is a metaphor for the human being.

The Kabbalistic Tree of Life is an attempt to describe the creation of the universe, and, simultaneously, it is an attempt to describe certain traits of the deity. The ten Sefirot of the Tree of Life are here listed in order from the beginning to the end:

1. Kether: Crown.
2. Chokhmah: Wisdom.
3. Binah: Understanding.
4. Chesed: Mercy.
5. Geburah: Judgment.
6. Tiphareth: Beauty.
7. Netzach: Victory.
8. Hod: Splendor.
9. Yesod: Foundation.
10. Malkuth: Kingdom.

In addition, as shown in the following figure, Daat (i.e., the "hidden Sefira" of knowledge) is the conceptual location (mystical state) where all ten Sefirot in the Tree of Life exist in their perfected state of mutual sharing.

The Kabbalistic Tree of Life

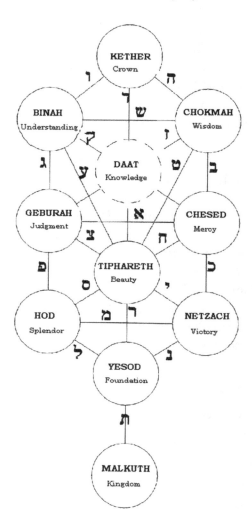

The highly influential science-fiction movie *The Matrix* (1999), creat-ed by the American film and TV directors, writers, and producers Lana Wachowski and Lilly Wachowski, follows a group of heroes who fight against mechanical overlords that have enslaved humanity in an extreme-ly sophisticated virtual-reality system. Thus, the term "Matrix" has been widely used in order to describe existential conditions that resemble the Platonic myth of the cave presented by Plato in his book *The Republic*

(Book 7, section 7) in order to illustrate "our nature in its education and want of education" (514a). In fact, this is the manner in which I use the term "Matrix" in this essay. Based on research works that I have published in my book entitled *Freemasonic Enlightenment* (Cambridge Scholars Publishing), I elucidate the Platonic myth of the cave, and I combine it with various mystics' quest for illumination. In this synoptic essay, based on my aforementioned book and the notes of a series of lectures that I have delivered in the Scholarly and Political Order of the Ur-Illuminati (SPOUI), of which I am the Grand Master, I shall present a Kabbalistic approach to the problem of "Matrix."

According to the Polish-Lithuanian Kabbalist Grand Master Jacob Frank (1726-91), originally named Jacob Leibowicz, who founded a mystical movement known as the Zoharists or Frankists, "all efforts of the ancestors were dedicated to this, that they might pursue that Maiden, upon whom the whole of life depended and who gives protection from all evil; no weapon has any power over men because of her help. Just as the Patriarchs dug a well" (Jacob Frank, "The Words of the Lord [Jacob Frank] from the Polish Manuscripts," edited, translated, and annotated by Harris Lenowitz, Professor of Hebrew, University of Utah, 124). The "Maiden" to whom Jacob Frank refers in the aforementioned passage of his "Words" is, according to him, the "Shekinah" and "Matronita": "Shekinah" is a Hebrew word that means the glory of the divine presence, and "Matronita" is a Greco-Spanish Kabbalistic term meaning Mother and Bride (ibid). Thus, Matronita is the Kabbalistic version of the term "Holy Goddess," referring specifically to the presence of the deity. Given that "Matronita" means Mother and Bride as well as "elder" and "younger," it signifies the Upper and the Lower Shekinah, or, in Hebrew, "Imma" (Mother) and "Kallah" (Bride). Therefore, when one refers to the Shekinah, "Imma" signifies the transcendent aspect of the Shekinah, and "Kallah" signifies the immanent aspect of the Shekinah, that is, our experience of the Shekinah. Moreover, in the previous case, the term "Kallah" is semantically interchangeable with the Hebrew term "Nukva" (meaning "[we] will be penetrated," in the sense that our mind will be filled with divine energy).

In the Bible, the mind as a repository of divine energy within the human being is referred to as the "neshamah," which literally means breath, and it can be broadly understood as the "soul proper" and the ability to become partakers of God. In the Bible, there are several references to the "neshamah," such as the following: Isaiah 30:33: breath of God as hot wind kindling a flame; 2 Samuel 22:16 and Job 4:9: as destroying wind; Job 32:8 and 33:4: as cold wind producing ice; 1 Kings 17:17, Isaiah 42:5, Job 27:3, and Daniel 10:7: breath of man; Genesis 2:7 and Job 34:14 and 36:4: breath of life and God's breath in man; Isaiah 2:22: man in whose nostrils is but a breath.

However, according to Rabbi Isaac (ben Solomon) Luria (1534-72), known also as "Ha-Ari Hakadosh" (The Holy Lion), who was one of the most influential Jewish mystics in the Galilee region of Ottoman Syria, and developed the so-called Lurianic Kabbalah (a school of Kabbalah named after him), the holy "Sefirot" (emanations), namely, the attributes/emanations through which the "Ein Sof" (the unmanifested Infinite Unity) reveals Itself and creates both the physical realm and the chain of higher spiritual realms, are surrounded by the unholy "Qliphoth." The Hebrew term "Qliphoth" literally means "Peels," "Shells," or "Husks" (the singular form "Qliphoth" is "Qlippah," and the singular form of "Sefirot" is "Sefira"). According to Isaac Luria's Biblical homilies and Kabbalistic system: "in essence, the Qlippah comes before holiness in every matter.... The parable of this is that the Qlippah of the stem is exceedingly beautiful but its entire end is Ha-Qlippah like it was said by Rashbi ["Zohar" 1:19]: 'This is Qlippah to that and this is nucleus to that'" (Ha-Ari Hakadosh, "Sefer Liquitim," Parshat Bereshit).

Therefore, the Lurianic Kabbalah differentiates the holy nucleus of the cosmos and of the beings and things that exist in the cosmos from their impure, unholy peel, and, in this way, it reveals important esoteric knowledge regarding Eden and the narrative of the Book of Genesis. One may find more details about these issues and the relation between Luria's mystical notion of "holy nucleus" and the Greek philosophical notion of "logos" (the efficient and final cause) in my book *Freemasonic Enlightenment* (Cambridge Scholars Publishing).

Using my method rational dynamicity, the ten Sefirot of the Kabbalistic Tree of Life underpin an anthropocentric synthesis between religion and science, between academic philosophy and esotericism, between spirit and matter, and, generally, between the reality of consciousness (which is, among other things, the realm of esoteric knowledge and magic) and the reality of the world (which is, among other things, the realm of exoteric knowledge). In particular, based on my method of rational dynamicity, I interpret Kether as a symbolic representation of the reality of being in general, I interpret the Left-hand Pillar of the Tree of Life as a symbolic representation of the reality of the world, I interpret the Right-hand Pillar of the Tree of Life as a symbolic representation of the reality of consciousness, and I interpret the Middle Pillar of the Tree of Life as a symbolic representation of the structural and dynamic continuity between the reality of consciousness and the reality of the world. Therefore, I propose the following correspondences:

1. Kether: the reality of being.

2. Chokhmah: the reality of consciousness.

3. Binah: the reality of the world.

4. Chesed: historical time.

5. Geburah: natural time.

6. Tiphareth: the dialectic of rational dynamicity.

7. Netzach: space as a creation of consciousness.

8. Hod: natural space.

9. Yesod: consciousness.

10. Malkuth: brain, or the central nervous system.

2.4 Hermeticism and Alchemy

A century after Alexander the Great conquered Egypt and founded his city, Alexandria, in 331 B.C., Greek settlers in Alexandria had begun to apply the epithet "megistos kai megistos theos megas" (greatest and greatest the great god) to Hermes and that this dignity derives from the epithet "two times great," which Egyptians had applied to Hermes's Egyptian equivalent, the god Thoth. The Greco-Egyptian Thoth-Hermes was the spirit of inventiveness. Sometime between the first century B.C. and the end of the first century A.D., a new figure appeared: "Hermes Trismegistus" (Thrice Greatest Hermes), a name with which Greek settlers in Egypt unified the Greek god Hermes and the Egyptian god Thoth since both were associated with magical knowledge, the dead, and healing. According to the Hermeticists' legends, the *Hermetica* was a collection of forty-two books of Greco-Egyptian magical wisdom that were written by Hermes Trismegistus, who was believed to be an ancient patriarch of civilization.

Along with the Kabbalah, the Hermetic tradition is one of the foundation stones on which modern esotericism is based. In particular, the Hermetic theorem "as above so below" underpins an "analogical" reasoning about an astrological ascent of the soul. This astrological ascent of the soul through celestial bodies is described in the first volume of the *Hermetica*, specifically, in the tractate that is called Poimandres. One can find hints to the concept of the soul's astrological ascent through the seven ancient astrological bodies (planets) in the myth of Er with which Plato concludes his *Republic* (10:614-10:621), and in the sixth book of Cicero's *De Re Publica*, where Cicero describes the dream vision of Scipio (Somnium Scipionis). Moreover, this concept can be found in the Kabbalah since the Kabbalistic Tree of Life shows an ascent through the following levels of consciousness and astrological bodies: Malkuth, which corresponds to the planet Earth; Yesod, which corresponds to the Moon; Hod, which corresponds to Mercury; Netzach, which corresponds to Venus; Tiphareth, which corresponds to the Sun; Geburah, which corresponds to Mars; Chesed, which corresponds to Jupiter; Binah, which corresponds to Saturn; Chokhmah, which corresponds to the Zodiac; and, finally, Kether, which corresponds to the "First Movement," or "First Whirling."

Western alchemy is intimately related to the resurgence of Hermeticism and Neoplatonic varieties of mysticism in the fifteenth and the sixteenth centuries A.D. According to Hermeticism, namely, the cult of Hermes Trismegistus,[10] the classical elements (earth, air, fire, water) make up the physical world, while the spiritual world (God, the One, the All) created the physical world by an act of will.[11] In particular, according to Hermetic cosmology, there is a reciprocal relationship between the physical world (the physical "microcosm") and the spiritual world (the spiritual "macrocosm"): the world is a beautiful whole, and creation can be understood by understanding that earthly realities imperfectly mirror supernatural realities, in accordance with the Hermetic maxim "as above, so below."

Sir Isaac Newton translated the Emerald Tablet – one of the most important pieces of the *Hermetica* reputed to contain the secret of the "prima materia" and its transmutation – as follows:

> 'Tis true without lying, certain most true. That which is below is
> like that which is above that which is above is like that which is

---

10   The *Hermetica* are Egyptian-Greek wisdom texts from the second and the third centuries A.D. that are mostly presented as dialogues in which a teacher, generally identified as Hermes Trismegistus ("thrice-greatest Hermes"), enlightens a disciple. These texts form the basis of Hermeticism.
11   Willis Barnstone, ed., *The Other Bible: Jewish Pseudepigrapha, Christian Apocrypha, Gnostic Scriptures, Kabbalah, Dead Sea Scrolls,* San Francisco: Harper, 2005.

below to do the miracles of one only thing. And as all things have been arose from one by the mediation of one: so all things have their birth from this one thing by adaptation. The Sun is its father, the moon its mother, the wind hath carried it in its belly, the earth its nurse. The father of all perfection in the whole world is here. Its force or power is entire if it be converted into earth. Separate thou the earth from the fire, the subtle from the gross sweetly with great industry. It ascends from the earth to the heaven again it descends to the earth and receives the force of things superior and inferior. By this means ye shall have the glory of the whole world thereby all obscurity shall fly from you. Its force is above all force. For it vanquishes every subtle thing and penetrates every solid thing. So was the world created. From this are and do come admirable adaptations whereof the means (or process) is here in this. Hence I am called Hermes Trismegist, having the three parts of the philosophy of the whole world. That which I have said of the operation of the Sun is accomplished and ended.[12]

The oldest known text of the Emerald Tablet has been dated to around the eighth century A.D. We can find it in two Arabic texts: the *Kitab-i Sirri Al-Halika*, which was written in the eighth century A.D. by the Arab polymath and alchemist Jabir ibn Hayyan (in the West, his name was Latinized into "Geber"), and the *Kitab Sirr Al-Asrar*, which was a tenth-century A.D. Arabic text translated into Latin in the twelfth century as the *Secretum Secretorum* (the Secret of Secrets). The Hermetic principle "as above, so below; as below, so above" refers to the interplay between spirit and matter as well as to the interplay between thought and form. In the language of alchemy, this principle is related to and represented by "distillation." Distillation is the process of separating the components or substances from a liquid mixture by using selective boiling and condensation (for instance, this is the method by which brandy and other "spirits" are produced): the alchemists refer to the gas that is let off during the phase of vaporization as the "spirit" (representing our thoughts and emotions), and they refer to the fixed matter that is produced during the phase of condensation as the "body." By analogy, nature has its own distillery: the heat of the Sun evaporates the water of the Earth, the water (moisture) goes up into the clouds, and then it rains. From the perspective of alche-

---

12   See: B. J. T. Dobbs, "Newton's Commentary on the Emerald Tablet of Hermes Trismegistus," in *Hermeticism and the Renaissance*, edited by Ingrid Merkel and Allen G. Debus, Washington: Folger Shakespeare Library; London: Associated University Presses, 1988, Part 2p. 183.

my, distillation and the Hermetic principle "as above, so below; as below, so above" mean that we continually create and manifest our world, and, therefore, magic is the power of consciously controlling what we send out; hence, Jesus Christ has said: "it is what comes out of a man that defiles him" (Mark 7:15). Therefore, the great problems of the Rosicrucian Science are the transmutation of the elements, the fixing of the volatile, and the volatilization of the fixed.

In the fifteenth and the sixteenth centuries A.D., the students of mysticism and the occult arts, such as Marsilio Ficino and Heinrich Cornelius Agrippa, were highly learned persons seeking to understand the reality of nature by means of the writings of ancient authorities, such as Plato, Pythagoras, and Hermes Trismegistus, and they believed that human reason was insufficient to provide humanity with the knowledge of the divine mysteries.[13]

The subject-matter of Alchemy plays a major role in Western esotericism, it has been handed down to us from the Sages of medieval Europe, and the latter obtained it from three principal sources, namely: First, from the Arabs, who almost alone preserved the Hermetic Art through the Middle Ages. Secondly, from Jewish rabbis, who possessed the traditional lore that is known as the Kabbalah. Thirdly, from the ancient Egypt of the Pharaohs, which was ruled by mighty priest-kings who were initiates in the Mysteries of Isis, Osiris, and Serapis. Therefore, at this point, it is apropos to contemplate Egyptian mythology.

According to Egyptian mythology, Ptah was the Egyptian god of Memphis and a divine defender of craftsmen and artists. He was credited with the invention of arts, and he was a metalworker and architect. From the perspective of the Kabbalistic Tree of Life, Ptah corresponds to Kether. Another important ancient Egyptian god of knowledge and illumination was Thoth. He was the divine Egyptian champion of science, music, literature, wisdom, and invention as well as the keeper of the divine Records. In Hermopolis, Thoth was believed to have hatched the Cosmic Egg: when Thoth first sang, the sound from his voice created four gods and four goddesses, who continued the world's creation by word and song. Moreover, he helped Isis to restore Osiris, he sustained the Child Horus, and he became the judge of Horus and Seth. From the perspective of the Kabbalistic Tree of Life, Thoth corresponds to Chokhmah.

---

13   See: Francis Barrett, *The Magus, Or Celestial Intelligence,* London: Lackington, Alley, and Co., 1801; Margery Purver, *The Royal Society: Concept and Creation*, Cambridge: M.I.T Press, 1967.

Isis was the first daughter of Geb (the Egyptian god of the Earth) and Nut (the Egyptian goddess of the Sky), and she was chosen by her oldest brother and husband, Osiris, to share the throne. From the perspective of the Kabbalistic Tree of Life, Isis corresponds to Binah. Osiris represented the spirit of vegetation, and, from the perspective of the Kabbalistic Tree of Life, he corresponds to Malkuth. Isis created marriage, she taught women to grow corn and weave clothes, and she taught men to cure disease. Their brother Seth killed Osiris, and, in several versions of the story, he dismembered Osiris's body. With the assistance of other deities, including Thoth and Anubis, Isis searched for the pieces of Osiris's body, and she reassembled it. Her efforts were the prototype for mummification. According to ancient Egyptian mythology, the god that invented mummification was Anubis, who was presiding over funerals and was directing the dead to the afterworld. From a Kabbalistic perspective, Anubis corresponds to the eighth Sefira of the Kabbalistic Tree of Life, namely, that of Hod, and the ninth Sefira of the Kabbalistic Tree of Life, namely, that of Yesod, corresponds to Shu, one of the primordial Egyptian gods, who was a personification of dry air. According to the Heliopolitan cosmology, Shu separated Nut from Geb as they were in the act of love, and, thus, he created duality in the manifest world. Ancient Greeks associated Shu with Atlas, the primordial Titan who held up the celestial spheres (in fact, "Shu" means "he who holds up").

Isis's love and grief for her husband Osiris and her powerful magical spells restored breath and life to Osiris's body. Isis copulated with Osiris and conceived their son Horus. However, from this point on, Osiris lives on only in the Duat, namely, the underworld. Horus is a solar god and is often identified with the ancient Greek god Apollo. From the perspective of the Kabbalistic Tree of Life, Horus as Lord of Force corresponds to Geburah, while Amoun, an ancient Egyptian god of expedition and discovery, corresponds to Chesed. In ancient Egyptian mythology, it is often mentioned that the wife of Horus was Hathor-Sekhmet, a female deity that can be identified with both the ancient Greek goddess of love, Aphrodite, and the Anatolian mother goddess Cybele, who ruled life and death. From the perspective of the Kabbalistic Tree of Life, Hathor-Sekhmet corresponds to Netzach.

The myth of Osiris symbolizes the human soul's drama. Osiris himself symbolizes the soul proper, namely, what in ancient Greek is called "nous," the repository of the uncreated spirit, or what the Kabbalists call "neshamah." Within the profane men, Osiris is dead through the lower nature, symbolized by Seth. Seth symbolizes the animal soul, particularly, selfish sentiments and passions. Thus, Osiris is buried in the shrine of the "mummy" of the materialistic world and thrown into the Nile, which symbolizes materialistic life. But Isis, who symbolizes the realm of the "sacred" and the love for the divine, that is, for the real truth, seeks, with the help of Anubis (who symbolizes divine wisdom) and Thoth (who symbolizes divine grace), the parts of Osiris's fragmented corpse (being), to reassemble them, thus giving rise to an integrated and spiritually revived harmonious soul, symbolized by Horus.

The cult of Serapis was introduced during the third century B.C. on the orders of the Greek Pharaoh Ptolemy I "the Savior" of the Ptolemaic Kingdom (a Hellenistic Kingdom based in ancient Egypt) as a means to unify the Greeks and the Egyptians in his realm. Serapis, depicted as Greek in appearance but with Egyptian trappings, was a syncretistic deity derived from the worship of the Egyptian gods Osiris and Apis (an intermediary between humans and Osiris), the Greek god Hades (the god of the dead and the king of the underworld), the Greek goddess Demeter (the goddess of grain, agriculture, harvest, growth, and nourishment), and the Greek god Dionysus (the god of the grape-harvest, wine, fertility, ritual madness, religious ecstasy, sacrifice, and theater).

Now, let's focus on the question of Alchemy. Alchemy has two aspects, specifically, the material and the spiritual. The opinion that Alchemy was only a primitive form of chemistry is untenable by anyone who has read the works of its most noted professors. The opinion that Alchemy was only a system of religious teachings, and that its chemical references were all mere allegories, is equally untenable, since many of the most noted professors of Alchemy made important discoveries in the scholarly discipline of chemistry, and they were in no way notable as teachers either of ethics or religion.

Chemistry, that is, the modern science that investigates the constitution of material substances, is the lineal descendant of Alchemy. The syllable "Al" is the Arabic definite article, meaning "The," and, therefore, Alchemy was "The Higher Chemistry." It was concerned with the study of the following issues:

- the essential nature of Matter,
- the Elements,

- metals,

- minerals, and

- Transmutation.

However, modern Chemistry is a science devoted chiefly to utilitarian and commercial purposes.

The term "transmutation" is an alchemical concept that means an attempt to understand the logoi of beings in order, ultimately, to purify and ontologically perfect material objects and humanity itself. Firstly, alchemy is related to the practices that were used in the Greco-Roman Egypt by goldsmiths and other artificers in metals, who had developed techniques for painting metals so as to make them look like gold. Secondly, alchemy is related to the theory of the unity of matter (originated by Greek Pre-Socratic philosophers), according to which all those things we are accustomed to call different kinds of matter were primordially derived from one primary kind of matter (in Latin, "prima materia"), whose alchemical symbol is the Ouroboros, namely, a serpent-dragon eating its own tail. Thirdly, alchemy is related to the Aristotelian principle that every art is and must be "mimesis," in the sense that, according to Aristotle's *Poetics*, 50a15, art "enmatters" species, and mimesis is "the constitution of things" (in Greek, "he ton pragmaton systasis"). Fourthly, alchemy is related to the ancient Greek concept of "cosmic sympathy," also symbolized by the Ouroboros. In the context of ancient Greek medicine, according to the *Hippocratic corpus* (*De alim.*, 23:1), sympathy refers to the relationship among different parts of the body, particularly, it refers to the fact that, when a part of the human body somehow suffers, another part may be affected, too. In the context of ancient Greek sociology, according to Aristotle's *Politics*, 1340a13, sympathy refers to the fact that people may share the feelings of their fellow-citizens. Moreover, during the Hellenistic period, Stoic philosophers, such as Chrysippus and Posidonius, developed the concept of "cosmic sympathy" in order to describe the interconnectedness among the different parts of the universe.

In the study of alchemy, practice and experiment are necessary, thus paving the road to modern natural science, but these need to be preceded by theoretical knowledge, which constitutes the philosophical or spiritual aspect of alchemy. In general, alchemy has two aspects: the material and the spiritual. The argument that alchemy was merely a primitive form of chemistry is untenable by anyone who is familiar with works written by its chief adepts. Additionally, the argument that alchemy is only a set of philosophical and theological teachings and that the alchemists' chemical references are only allegories is equally untenable by anyone who is familiar with the history of alchemy, since many of alchemy's most prominent adepts have made significant contributions to chemistry, and they have not been notable as teachers either of philosophy or of theology; in Antoine-Joseph Pernety's *Dictionnaire Mytho-Hermétique* (Paris: Delalain, 1758), one can find a very important explanation of alchemical terms upon the material plane.

The most ancient known alchemist is the Greek alchemist Zosimos of Panopolis, who flourished in the Greco-Roman Egypt in the late third century A.D. and in the early fourth century A.D. The tenth-century A.D. Byzantine encyclopedic dictionary *Souda* writes that "chemeia," from which alchemy (in Greek, "alchemeia") is derived, is the art of making silver and gold (the two so-called perfect metals), thus emphasizing the practical aspect of alchemy.[14] Additionally, according to the *Souda*'s lemma "chemeia," the Roman Emperor Diocletian (who reigned from 284 to 305 A.D.) burned several alchemical books that existed in Egypt and contained information about the art of making silver and gold because he did not want the Egyptians to accumulate wealth through the practice of alchemy, and because he was afraid that the Egyptians would be empowered and emboldened by the practice of alchemy.

Byzantine scholars maintain that alchemy has two aspects: the material and the spiritual. For instance, the Byzantine rhetorician Aineias Gazaios (fifth/sixth century A.D.), in his philosophical dialogue entitled *Theophrastus*, tries to explain the resurrection of bodies on the Judgment Day through the divine Creator's art, according to which the body and the soul are united integrally, and, for this purpose, Aineias Gazaios draws examples from the practice of alchemy.[15] In particular, in his *Theophrastus*, Aineias Gazaios refers to the art of transmutation, by which it was sought to produce silver and gold from other, less precious metals, while, with regard to spiritual alchemy, Aineias Gazaios delineates transmutation as an art that leads to the spiritualization of matter and the salvation of the psychosomatic nexus of the human being. It is important to mention that,

---

14   Herbert Hunger, *Die Hochsprachliche profane Literatur der Byzantiner*, vol. 2, München: Beck, 1978.

15   Enea Di Gaza, *Teofrasto*, Napoli: Salvatore Iodice, 1958.

in contrast to radically dualistic approaches to spiritual alchemy, which reflect an Asian world-negating mentality craving for the liberation of spirit from the material world, the purpose of the Byzantine approach to spiritual alchemy is to guide the human being as an integral union of mind and body towards the actualization of humanity's divine potential.

In the Middle Ages and in the Renaissance, both material and spiritual alchemy expanded throughout the Islamic world and Western Europe, and various alchemical "schools" were developed by Arab, Persian, and Western European alchemists, such as: Al-Farabi (born in Damascus, in the ninth century A.D.), Ibn Umayl (a tenth-century A.D. Arab alchemist who amalgamated Greek alchemy with Islamic spirituality), Al-Tughra'i (a Persian alchemist born in Isfahan, in the eleventh century A.D.; his alchemical texts incorporated extensive excerpts from earlier Arabic alchemical writings and Arabic translations of Zosimos of Panopolis's Greek alchemical treatises), Roger Bacon (a thirteenth-century English philosopher and Franciscan friar), the famous Swiss physician Paracelsus (born Theophrastus von Hohenheim, 1493-1541), etc.

Ethan Allen Hitchcock's *Remarks upon Alchemy and the Alchemists* (1857) is one of the most important Western sources for the study of the history and the meaning of alchemy. From the perspective of modern chemistry, an "element" is defined as a body that is substantially different from all others, while having constant character itself, and that it is indivisible except into parts of itself. However, the alchemists' elements, namely, Fire, Air, Earth, and Water, are types of four modes of force or matter, and they represent states that are mutually related and dependent, in accordance with the aforementioned ancient Greek concept of "cosmic sympathy." In particular, in the context of alchemy, the following correspondences hold:

Fire–Heat–Dryness

Air–Heat–Moistness

Earth–Cold–Dryness

Water–Cold–Moistness

The aforementioned alchemical correspondences are based on Aristotle's natural philosophy, according to which matter, simple or combined with its developments, may exist in each of these states.

Apart from the aforementioned four elementary states, the alchemists refer to minerals and seven metals, as forms of matter that are essentially stable, except in the hands of an adept alchemist, who might accomplish the Great Work, that is, the transmutation of one of them into another. For the alchemical process of transmutation, one substance was requisite, precisely, the Philosopher's Stone, known also as the Quintessence and as the Son of the Sun. This was to be derived from the Philosophical Mercury, the Philosophical Salt, and the Philosophical Sulfur, which, by putrefaction or calcination, became Black, and then, by further processes, White, and, finally, the Redness of Perfection was achieved. In medieval alchemical texts, the sublimation or volatilization of a substance is called the White Eagle, whereas the Black Eagle refers to putrefaction, by which is meant conversion by heat of dissolved substances or liquids into a form of sediment or precipitate, or of melted substances into slag or a form of ashes. Thus, one of the most well-known alchemical principles is "Solve et Coagula," meaning either dissolve and precipitate from solution, or melt and solidify. The aforementioned Philosopher's Stone was the Key to Transmutation, since, according to the alchemists, by the power of the Philosopher's Stone, one form of matter could be changed into another: Lead could be transmuted into Silver, called by them the Moon (in Latin, "Luna") or the Queen, while Silver could be transmuted into Gold, called by them the Sun (in Latin, "Sol") or the King.[16]

On the symbolic and philosophical planes, the alchemical principle "Solve et Coagula," that is, "volatilize and fix," can be interpreted as follows: the fallen soul becomes fixed in matter, and, particularly, the mind that is coagulated and fettered by the sensuous world suffers the consequent loss of the power of direct spiritual communion with God; by mystical death, precisely, by being dead to the sensuous world, and by casting off the body's animal passions, the mind is released from its bondage and becomes a partaker of God's uncreated energies. The alchemical principles Sun and Moon, which, in chemistry, correspond to Gold and Silver, respectively, symbolize the soul and the body of man, respectively. The alchemical principles of Mercury, Salt, and Sulfur symbolize the active principle, the passive principle, and their synthesis, respectively. Furthermore, when alchemists maintain that, by time and

16   Important aspects of the so-called Higher Alchemy have been illustrated by Anna Kingsford (1846–88) and her co-worker Edward Maitland. Moreover, see: Louis Figuier, *L'Alchimie et les Alchimistes*, Paris: Hachette, 1856 (reprinted by Éditions Denoël, Paris, 1970); and Albert Poisson, *Théorie et Symboles des Alchimistes: Le Grand Oeuvre*, Paris: Éditions Maçonniques de France, 2014.

force, the Black Dragon of putrefaction can become fashioned into the White Swan of purity, they refer to a mental change (in Greek, "metanoia"), precisely, to the return of the mind to the heart and the liberation of the mind from bodily sensation.

2.5 The Renaissance

The Renaissance led European civilization to modernity, combining elements of the medieval civilization and new findings. The term "Renaissance" was coined by the French historian Jules Michelet (1798-1874), who used it in his seminal book *Histoire de France* (vol. 7, Paris: Librairie Internationale A. Lacroix & Cie., 1876) in order to describe the historical period that roughly covers the time from 1400 to 1600 as "the discovery of the world, the discovery of man." The Renaissance was guided by the idea of reviving classical Antiquity, but it attempted to do so in a creative and unique way that was underpinned by the post-medieval human being's self-confidence and humanistic spirit. Hence, the Renaissance is associated with the following events:

- the founding of Italian republics;

- the development of political science by the Italian diplomat, political philosopher, and writer Niccolò Machiavelli;

- the placing of emphasis on the principle of harmony (methodically studied by the Spanish mathematician, music theorist, and composer Bartolomé Ramos de Pareja, as well as by the Italian music theorists and composers Franchinus Gaffurius, Giovanni Spataro, and Pietro Aaron);

- the synthesis between Christian mysticism, Kabbalistic thought, and Neoplatonic philosophy by the Italian Renaissance scholar Giovanni Pico della Mirandola, who introduced the Kabbalah to the emerging Renaissance Neoplatonists and presented his seventy-two Kabbalistic *Conclusiones* as a way of confirming the Christian religion starting with the fundamentals of the Jewish spirituality;

- the development of the idea that the universe is infinite (proposed by the Italian Dominican friar, philosopher, and mathematician Giordano Bruno);

- the invention of the mechanical movable type printing press (by the German goldsmith and printer Johannes Gutenberg);

- the manufacturing of high-quality gunpowder and fire-arms;

- the construction and the systematic use of the nautical (magnetic) compass;

- the achievement of important advances in machinery, mining, and chemistry (as exemplified in Georg Bauer's treatise *De Re Metallica*, published in 1556);

- the rigorous formulation of Heliocentrism (i.e., the astronomical model in which the Earth and other planets revolve around the Sun at the center of the solar system; this astronomical model was originally proposed by the ancient Greek astronomer and mathematician Aristarchus of Samos, and it was reformulated in a scientifically more rigorous way by the Polish mathematician and astronomer Nicolaus Copernicus);

- the Lutheran Reformation (despite the fact that Martin Luther's teaching about the three "Solae" has caused agitation and controversies, Martin Luther's attempt was focused on liberating Western Christians from legalism and from a feeling of guilt that was deliberately cultivated by particular authoritarian clerical elites, and, therefore, he emphasized that the primary and most important factor that determines whether one can achieve eternal life is one's psychical openness towards Christ, the belief that God comes to serve humanity)[17];

- and the mastering of perspective space and perspective drawing (Renaissance artists replaced the extra-temporal and extra-spatial symbolism of medieval painting with the subject's own logical way of seeing the world).

2.6 Rosicrucianism

In essence, Rosicrucianism is not a particular Order, but a spiritual and cultural movement. The legendary history of the Rosicrucians goes back to medieval Germany. The earliest public notice of the Fratres of the Rose and Cross appeared in 1614 in a pamphlet printed at Kassel in Germany and entitled *Fama Fraternitatis Rosae Crucis* (The Fame of the

Fraternity of the Rose and Cross). In 1615, a new edition of the previous pamphlet appeared, to which was added another one, entitled *Confessio Fraternitatis* (The Confession of the Fraternity), giving great promises about future revelations. The following year saw the publication of a new Rosicrucian manifesto entitled the *Chymical Wedding of Christian Rosenkreutz*, whose authorship is attributed to Johann Valentin Andreae, a Lutheran theologian from Tübingen, and it describes the path to salvation through ecstasy and enlightenment. Andreae's work immediately attracted the attention of alchemists, theosophists, doctors, and astrologers, who founded Rosicrucian fraternities not only in Germany but also in France, Austria, England, and the Netherlands. In 1652, the Welsh mystical philosopher and alchemist Thomas Vaughan, who was writing under the pseudonym of Eugenius Philalethes, translated the aforementioned Rosicrucian pamphlets into English.

The *Fama Fraternitatis* starts as follows:

> Seeing the only Wise and Merciful God in these latter days hath poured out so richly his mercy and goodness to Mankind, whereby we do attain more and more to the perfect knowledge of his Son Jesus Christ and Nature, that justly we may boast of the happy time, wherein there is not only discovered unto us the half part of the World, which was heretofore unknown and hidden, but he hath also made manifest unto us many wonderful, and never heretofore seen, Works and Creatures of Nature, and moreover hath raised men endued with great Wisdom, which might partly renew and reduce all Arts (in this our Age spotted and imperfect) to perfection; so that finally Man might thereby understand his own Nobleness and Worth, and why he is called *Microcosmus*, and how far his knowledge extendeth in Nature. (italics in original)

The *Fama Fraternitatis* announced the existence of a discreet fraternity founded in the late Middle Ages by a German nobleman, the "pious, spiritual, and highly-illuminated Father" Fr. C.R. (most probably meaning Christian Rosenkreutz). According to the *Fama*, dissatisfied with monastic life, the young C.R. travelled with a Father P.A.L. to the East in search of knowledge, and he reached Cyprus, where his friend died in 1393. Brother C.R. then went on to Damascus, where he conducted further studies, and, subsequently, he went to Egypt, where he remained for a long time. He journeyed along the Mediterranean Sea and visited Fez, where he studied the accumulated scientific and philosophical knowledge as well as the magic, that is, the alchemical treatises, of the Arabs.

In fact, by the late Middle Ages, the Arabs and the Persians had already created big libraries, and they had collected and translated many ancient Greek philosophical and scientific books. During the reign of the Abbasid caliphs al-Mansur (754-75 A.D.) and Harun al-Rashid (786-809 A.D.), many works of ancient Greek philosophers and scientists, such as Aristotle, Hippocrates, Galen of Pergamon, Ptolemy, and Euclid, were translated into Arabic by such prominent translators and scholars as Ibn Bakhtishu, Theodore Abu Qurrah, al-Bitriq, and his son Yahya, etc. The Abbasid caliph al-Mamun (reign: 813-33 A.D.), son of Harun al-Rashid, supported the study of ancient Greek philosophy and science, and he was an advocate of philosophical free thinking. Moreover, in Baghdad, caliph Harun al-Rashid founded an intellectual center called the "House of Wisdom" (in Arabic, Bayt al-Hikma), which was generously sponsored and developed further by caliph al-Mamun.

Finally, Brother C.R. crossed over into Spain, where he learned the Jewish Kabbalah and the philosophy of the Moors. It is worth pointing out that the Moors were the first great improvers of natural sciences in medieval Western Europe since they had acquired their sciences from the Greeks through the Byzantine Empire, and they created renowned universities in Spain, such as those of Seville, Cordova, and Granada; "and such was the reputation which they had acquired, that crowds of learned men from various countries resorted to Spain to study those sciences."[17] During his journey in search of wisdom, Brother C.R. observed how the Eastern sages shared their knowledge without jealousy, hypocrisy, or egoism.

In 1402, Brother C.R. returned to Germany, and he settled down to codify the vast amount of knowledge that he had collected. However, in Germany, he found only hostility and indifference. Thus, in Germany, in a place now unknown, Brother C.R. established a fraternity of sympathetic brethren, namely, the Fratres R.C., who met annually in secret in the "House of the Holy Spirit," as they called their assembly, with the aim to advance science and an esoteric approach to religion, and to further a deep reformation of knowledge.

Six ordinances were laid down to govern the original members of the Rosicrucian Fraternity in the conduct of their lives, namely:

---

17   *The Edinburgh Encyclopedia*, vol. 17, p. 388.

1. None of them should profess any great powers, knowledge, or authority to the outer world, but they should do good and heal the poor freely.

2. No peculiar habit should be worn when out in the world to make them conspicuous or liable to persecution.

3. On one day at least in every year all Fratres should assemble to record their work and communicate to each other their gains of knowledge.

4. Every Frater should seek one or more suitable persons to succeed him.

5. "R.C." or "C.R." should be their seal, mark, and character.

6. The Fraternity should remain a secret or private one, at least for a hundred years, if not longer.

Around 1450, the eldest Fratres or Magistri designed and executed a funeral Chamber in which Brother C.R. should be buried when his end came. Brother C.R. died in 1484, and he was entombed. On the door of the vault the inscription "Post centum viginti annos patebo" was engraved on a brazen plate, meaning that the vault should be opened after 120 years. This long period passed by, and, even though Roman Catholicism had been fiercely attacked by the Religious Reformation, the work of the Rosicrucians had continued in peace and secrecy. In 1604, the Fratres then forming the central group of the Rosicrucian Fraternity disclosed the door of the secret chamber and entered the vault, where the Founder's body was lying in perfect condition, clothed in the symbolic robe and the insignia of his office of Magus (i.e., Head) of the Fraternity, and there were found stored the original books and achievements of the earliest members.

Through the aforementioned symbols and allegorical language, the original Rosicrucian manifestos, namely, the *Fama* and the *Confessio*, are concerned with the following goal: the union of religion and science in the context of a spiritual quest for the real truth of both the visible and the invisible things. This is the context in which Rosicrucians study mysticism, specifically, Hermetic philosophy, Alchemy (also known as the Hermetic Art), and the Kabbalah; they delve into the natural sciences, they promote the development of science, in general, and, simultaneously, they cultivate an esoteric approach to religion. The unifying principle that pervades the entire spectrum of the Rosicrucians' endeavors is their attempt to grasp (and partake of) the one, ultimate source of the meaning of all beings and things, visible and invisible.

2.7 Freemasonry

In its broadest sense, Symbolic, or Speculative, Masonry is an initiatory organization that uses symbols and allegories related to Operative Masonry in order to teach morality and transmit moral virtue, to dramatize philosophical ideas, and to forge fraternal relations between its members. However, beyond the previous general definition of Symbolic Masonry, each particular Body of Symbolic Masonry has its own "landmarks" and ethos. Thus, for instance, the United Grand Lodge of England, the Grand Orient of France, The International Order of Co-Freemasonry Le` Droit Humain, the Swedish Order of Freemasonry, and other Orders of Symbolic Masonry comply with the previous generic definition of Symbolic Masonry, but each one of them has its own distinct and exclusive landmarks and/or initiatory customs and rituals. In other words, like the market of construction companies, which is pluralistic and competitive, the market of symbolic construction companies, namely, of Symbolic Masonic Orders, is pluralistic and competitive, too.

Giuliano Di Bernardo (who served as the Grand Master of the Grand Orient of Italy (Grande Oriente d'Italia) from 1990 to 1993 and as the Founding Grand Master of the Regular Grand Lodge of the Ancient Free and Accepted Masons of Italy (Gran Loggia Regolare degli Antichi Liberi e Accettati Muratori d'Italia) from 1993 to 2001) has summarized the generic characteristics of Freemasonry as follows.[18]

> First of all, it is necessary to distinguish the concepts of Freemasonry into *initiatory* and *profane*. Initiatory concepts are those whose meaning is known only to Masons, while profane concepts are those whose meaning is understandable even to non-Masons.
>
> The initiatory concept par excellence is that of a "secret," while the fundamental profane concepts are those of "freedom," "tolerance," "brotherhood," "transcendence."
>
> The fundamental secular concepts of Freemasonry (liberty, tolerance, brotherhood, transcendence) are essential elements of the

---

18   It is included in an essay that Professor and Freemasonic Grand Master Giuliano Di Bernardo contributed to my volume *Freemasonic Enlightenment*.

Masonic philosophical anthropology, that is, of the model of man as conceived by Freemasonry. To use a technical expression, we say that they represent a set of four elements that we call "quadruple" and that we indicate as follows: "Freedom, Tolerance, Brotherhood, Transcendence."

In the British Museum, there is an old document of about 1390 that gives some rules and regulations, or, as they are known among Freemasons, "Charges." This document is called the *Regius Poem*,[19] and it is admitted to be the oldest genuine record of Masonry known. The Charges contained in the *Regius Poem* indicate that Masonry was not only a technical activity, but simultaneously it was organized in such a manner that it safeguarded and promoted a specific civil ethos. Thus, from the very beginning, Masonry was a civilizing force founded on the culture that underpinned the creation of the first medieval towns in Western Europe. The fact that Masonry has a cultural core, which transcends the technical activities of Operative Masons, led to the creation and survival of Freemasonry as a symbolic system, namely, as a cultural phenomenon, after the decay of the guild system.

In Scotland, historians found several trustworthy historical sources on lodges of stonemasons (that is, Operative Masons). Lodges were geographically-defined units controlling the operative trade on the basis of their statute law. On 28 December 1598 and also on 28 December 1599, William Schaw (1550-1602) – who, in 1583, was appointed the King's Master of Works[20] (by King James VI of Scotland) – drew up the documents that today are known as the First and the Second Schaw Statutes, and they include instructions to Scottish stonemasons' lodges on practical matters concerning Operative Masonry. However, the Schaw Statutes include also instructions that have a cultural and, particularly, moral character – for example: "that they be true to one another, live charitably together as becometh sworn brethren and companions of Craft"; and: "that they observe and keep all the good ordinances set down before con-

---

19   For the complete original text, see: *Constituciones Artis Geometriae Secundum Euclydem*, with introductory remarks by H. J. Whymper, London: Spencer & Co., Great Queen Street, 1889. The modern English translation was made by Roderick H. Baxter, Past Master of Quatuor Coronati Lodge, No. 2076, under the auspices of the United Grand Lodge of England, and it is reproduced by: A. G. Mackey, *Encyclopedia of Freemasonry*, new and revised edition, New York and London: The Masonic History Company, 1914. See also: S. H. Sheperd, *The Landmarks of Freemasonry*, Whitefish, MT: Kessinger Publishing, 1997.

20   On 21 December 1583, James VI appointed him principal Master of Works in Scotland for life, with responsibility for all royal castles and palaces. See: *Register of the Privy Seal of Scotland, 1581-1584*, Vol. 8, No. 1676, 1982, pp. 276-277.

cerning the privileges of their craft as set down by their predecessors of fond memory."

Furthermore, historians are now certain that Scottish operative lodges began, in the seventeenth century, to admit non-operative members as "Accepted," meaning honorary or gentlemen, Masons, and that, by the early eighteenth century, the Accepted Masons had gained the ascendancy.[21] The lodges in which the Accepted Masons had gained the ascendancy became symbolic, or "speculative," lodges, while others continued practicing Operative Masonry. The speculative, or symbolic, Scottish lodges eventually combined to form the Grand Lodge of Scotland in 1736.

---

21   See: John Hamill, *The Craft: History of English Freemasonry*, London: Aquarian Press, 1986.

CHAPTER 3

THE MODERN AND PERFECTING RITE OF SYMBOLIC MASONRY

DEGREES:

The degrees of the Autonomous Order of the Modern and Perfecting Rite of Symbolic Masonry are:

Entered Apprentice:

It teaches various important aspects of Freemasonry's history and philosophy, psychology, and philosophy.

Fellow Craft:

It teaches philosophy, science, politology, and political economy.

Master Mason:

It is focused on psychoanalysis, and it includes an important Charge concerned with comparative studies of Masonic Orders and rituals, which I quote below. I have personally written this lecture (as well as all the rituals, the catechisms, the lectures, and the charges of the three degrees of the Modern and Perfecting Rite of Symbolic Masonry) in such a way that, in the form of a dialogue, it informs the newly raised Master Mason of the history of various Masonic rituals and currents.

STRUCTURE:

The officers of a Lodge of the Autonomous Order of the Modern and Perfecting Rite of Symbolic Masonry are:

Venerable Master
Senior Overseer
Junior Overseer
Organist
Director of Ceremonies
Secretary
Treasurer
Expert
Assistant Director of Ceremonies
Director of Music (or Orator)
Inner Guard
Outer Guard

The Charge of the Third Degree of the Modern and Perfecting Rite of Symbolic Masonry (excerpt)

"**Venerable Master:** Brother/Sister ... (*name and surname of the Candidate*), your raising to the sublime and supreme degree of a Master Mason reflects the dedication you have displayed for our Order over a long period of time and through several tests and tasks; and I do congratulate you most heartily.

According to our Order, a true Master Mason is an emissary of Light, the epicenter of an earthquake that destroys rotten and crumbling creations of human imperfection, the strong medicine that fights dementia, and the acid that washes away the filth of perversion and irrationality. Moreover, a Master Mason of the Modern and Perfecting Rite of Symbolic Masonry is a genuine expert in Masonic history and in the comparative study of Masonic rituals. For this reason, we shall teach you every significant element of the history and the rituals of the English Symbolic Masonry of the eighteenth and the nineteenth centuries, since the United Grand Lodge of England is the oldest Grand Lodge in the world and has played a major role in the shaping of the Craft. Furthermore, we shall teach you every significant element of the history and the rituals of the Ancient and Accepted Scottish Rite, which was formed and instituted in the U.S.A. during the eighteenth and the nineteenth centuries, since the Southern Masonic Jurisdiction of the U.S.A. is the oldest Supreme Council of the Ancient and Accepted Scottish Rite in the world and has played a major role in the attempt of several Masons to expand and enrich the basic English system of Symbolic Masonry with appendant Orders and degrees.

The Autonomous Order of the Modern and Perfecting Rite of Symbolic Masonry has reformed Symbolic Masonry in such a way that the Master Mason degree has absorbed and contains within it every important teaching of the Ancient and Accepted Scottish Rite. Thus, we shall offer you a complete, accurate, and synoptic exposition of all the wisdom of the English Symbolic Masonry as well as of all the degrees of the Ancient and Accepted Scottish Rite, given that our Order expresses a transition from old ritualism and mythology to philosophy and psychoanalysis.

Senior Overseer (S.O.): Even though Freemasonry already existed before the eighteenth century, the year 1717 signals the commencement of a new system of Freemasonic organization and government, namely, the "Grand Lodge" system. In particular, the "Grand Lodge of London and Westminster," also known as the "Premier Grand Lodge of England," was conceived and established on St. John the Baptist's day, 24 June 1717, by the following four Symbolic Lodges:

1. The Goose and Gridiron, St. Paul's Churchyard, established 1691,

2. Crown Ale House Lodge, Lincoln's Inn Fields, established 1712,

3. The Apple Tree Tavern, Covent Garden, now known as the Lodge of Fortitude and Old Cumberland, and

4. The Rummer and Grapes, Channel Row, Westminster, later known as Horn Lodge.

The first three Grand Masters of the Grand Lodge of London and Westminster were the following: Anthony Sayer, "a Gentleman," who was elected in 1717; George Payne, who was elected in 1718, and he was appointed Secretary to the Tax Office in 1732 and Head Secretary in 1743; and the Rev. Dr. John Theophilus Desaguliers, who was elected in 1719, and who was later three times Deputy Grand Master.

In 1713, the Parliament of Westminster invited George, the Electorate of Hanover and a Protestant, to be crowned King George I of Great Britain and

Ireland. Thus, King George I became the first British monarch of the House of Hanover, which succeeded the House of Stuart and the House of Orange.

In the Middle Ages, the Church was the quintessence of the State, and the civil authority was perceived to be a law enforcement apparatus of the Church. In Western Europe, by the end of the fourth century, the Church was using the secular arm of the Roman Empire in order to bring pagans and Christian sectarians into the Church of Rome. Given that the Church was the main repository of educated thought and opinion at every level of society, the clergy played protagonist roles in the kingdoms and other feudal entities. However, from the eleventh century, there was a slow trend in Western Europe towards the strengthening of feudal states and the development within them of new increasingly independent elites. Thus, gradually, Christian subjects lose their sense of dual allegiance to the "regnum" (royal authority) and the "sacerdotium" (papal authority), and then civil rulers maintain that they could exercise power without having to defer to papal authority. In 1534, King Henry VIII of England, by his Act of Supremacy, established a state Church, the Church of England, which mainly maintained the religious doctrines of the Roman Catholic Church, but was independent from the Pope. This change in the balance of power between civil and ecclesiastical authority was reinforced in the seventeenth century by the House of Stuart. In the seventeenth century, the House of Stuart united the Kingdoms of England and Scotland, and, thus, it formed the first United Kingdom. The United Kingdom was the first great European kingdom that became independent from the Pope's rule. Even though the Stuarts were Roman Catholic, they wanted to strengthen the king's power vis-à-vis the Papacy. Moreover, the Protestant Reformation marks the period in which the doctrine of the Two Swords, according to which the Pope possessed both swords but had granted the temporal sword to kings and other feudal lords, was replaced by the doctrine of the sovereign State, acknowledging the absolute, secular sovereignty of the ruler.

James VII and II of the House of Stuart, who was king of England and king of Ireland as James II and king of Scotland as James VII, converted to Roman Catholicism, favored a policy of religious tolerance rather than the prerogatives of the Church of England, promoted an alliance between the United Kingdom and the Catholic French royal house, questioning the established balance of power and the Papacy's interests in Continental Europe, and his second wife, Mary of Modena, gave birth to a son who was to be brought up as Roman Catholic. Thus, opposition against James VII and II was raised both among the Anglican establishment and the Roman Catholic establishment. In the context of the Glorious Revolution, which broke out in 1688, the English Parliament deposed James VII and II in favor of his Protestant daughters, Mary II, who co-reigned with her Dutch husband William of Orange from 1689 until her death in 1694, and Ann, who succeeded William of Orange after his death in 1702. Neither Queen Mary II nor Queen Ann had any children who survived to adulthood. Therefore, under the Act of Settlement, an Act of the English Parliament that was passed in 1701, excluding all Roman Catholics, Ann was succeeded by her second cousin George I of the House of Hannover. After the loss of the throne, the descendants of James VII and II came to be known as the Jacobites and continued to reclaim the Scottish and English throne as the rightful heirs.

George I of the House of Hannover was keen to eliminate every Jacobite element from British Freemasonry. In the context of the previous policy of Masonic "purity," the Premier Grand Lodge of Georgian England forbade all religious and political discussions within Masonic Lodges. Under the Hanoverian dynasty, every element that sustained prior, namely, pre-Hanoverian, forms of Freemasonic activity was declining or was buried deep below the surface. Hanoverian Freemasonry maintains that the keystone of the Freemasonic system is the principle of tolerance, and it mainly reflects the ethos of the Whig Party and the bourgeois establishment. In general, the Whigs were aligned with commercial interests and Protestant Dissenters (namely, Protestants who separated from the Church of England during the seventeenth and the eighteenth centuries), whereas the Tories favored the interests of the landed nobility and were supportive of the Anglican Church.

Based on actual Biblical references about the construction of King Solomon's Temple and on his Calvinist ethics, the Rev. Dr. John Theophilus Desaguliers, who was a French-born Huguenot clergyman closely aligned with the Hanoverian dynasty, articulated the following didactic story that was to become the major allegorical theme of the Third Degree within the Jurisdiction of the Grand Lodge of London and Westminster: Being knowledgeable in architecture and in metallurgy, Hiram Abiff was sent by Hiram King of Tyre, to Solomon King of Israel, to direct the construction of the Temple at Jerusalem, which the Israelites intended to erect to the glory of the Great Architect of the Universe. Hiram Abiff divided his workmen into three groups: Apprentices, Companions, and Masters. To be able to distinguish and recognize each group, he gave it its own set of secrets, precisely, a Word, a Sign, and a Grip. The works drawing to their close, three impious Companions ("ruffians"), having been unable to obtain the secrets of a Master, decided to extract the Sign, the Word, and the Grip of a Master from Hiram Abiff by any means. When Hiram Abiff finished his devotions, he moved towards the South entrance of the Temple, where he was opposed by the first impious Companion, who was armed with a heavy Plumb Rule and demanded the secrets of a Master, warning Hiram Abiff that he would die if he refused to comply with those impious and unworthy Masons' request. Hiram Abiff refused to divulge the secrets of a Master Mason without the consent and co-operation of Solomon King of Israel and Hiram King of Tyre, and he added that patience and industry would, in due time, entitle every worthy Mason to a participation of the secrets of a Master Mason. The impious Companion struck Hiram Abiff a violent blow on the right temple. When Hiram Abiff recovered from the shock, he moved towards the North entrance of the Temple, where he was opposed by the second impious Companion, who was armed with a Level. After Hiram Abiff gave a similar answer to the second impious Companion, the latter struck him a violent blow on the left temple. Hiram Abiff, "faint and bleeding," moved towards the East entrance of the Temple, where he was opposed by the third impious Companion, who was armed with a Maul. After Hiram Abiff gave a similar answer to the third impious Companion, the latter struck him a violent blow on the forehead, which was fatal.

According to the United Grand Lodge of England, the aforementioned Hiramic legend ritual completed the Order of the Holy Royal Arch of Jerusalem, which, according to the United Grand Lodge of England's Constitution, is the completion of the degree of a Master Mason. According to the Emulation Ritual, due to the untimely death of Hiram Abiff, the genuine secrets of a Master Mason are lost and cannot be communicated to any Freemason, since, without the consent and co-operation of the three Grand Masters, namely, Solomon King of Israel, Hiram King of Tyre, and Hiram Abiff, they could never be divulged. However, according to the United Grand Lodge of England, the genuine secrets of a Master Mason are restored in the Order of the Holy Royal Arch of Jerusalem.

The Royal Arch degree originally appeared in 1743, precisely, in *Faulkner's Dublin Journal*, dated 10-14 January 1743, where an article reported that "Youghall" Lodge No. 21 celebrated St. John's Day with a parade in which there was "the Royal Arch carried by two excellent Masons." In 1744, in Dublin, Ireland, Fifield D'Assigny published a book entitled *A Serious and Impartial Enquiry into the Cause of the Present Decay of Freemasonry in the Kingdom of Ireland*, in which he argued that the Royal Arch degree was conferred in Dublin "some few years ago," and that it had been brought there from the city of York. The ceremony of "exaltation" to the Royal Arch is based on the legend of the rebuilding of King Solomon's Temple after the Babylonian Captivity, in the sixth century B.C.

Babylonian Captivity, also called Babylonian Exile, is the forced detention of Jews in Babylon, following the destruction of Jerusalem by Nebuchadnezzar in ca. 586 B.C. The exile formally ended in ca. 538 B.C., when the Persian conqueror of Babylon, Cyrus the Great, gave the Jews permission to return to Palestine. The Biblical book of Ezra narrates the history of the Jewish exiles' return to Jerusalem and of the construction of the second Jerusalem Temple. In ca. 536 B.C., Zerubbabel, who was the grandson of Jechonias, penultimate king of Judah, led the people in rebuilding the altar and laying the second Jerusalem Temple's foundation.

According to the English Royal Arch's allegorical narrative, Jewish captives returning to Jerusalem, after the Babylonian Captivity, participate in the reconstruction of the Jerusalem Temple, and, while constructing the Second Temple of Jerusalem, they discover a large underground *vault* consisting of nine arches. Within this vault, they discover the true name of God, namely, YEHOVAH (Jehovah), engraved on a golden plate that they found atop a triangular pedestal that was placed under the keystone of the ninth arch. This discovery marks the rediscovery of the long-lost genuine secrets of a Master Mason, according to the Order of the Holy Royal Arch of Jerusalem.

The symbolic meaning of the aforementioned discovery is the following: what was lost by King Solomon and most of his successors for the next four centuries was the genuine metaphysical secrets of Biblical Judaism and, more particularly, the belief that Yehovah was the one and only true God of Israel. What was found by the time the captives returned to Jerusalem was an even broader awareness than the one which was lost: the exiles re-discovered the truth that Yehovah was the one and only true

God of Israel, and that Yehovah was not merely the God of a specific nation, that is, Yehovah was not only the God of Israel among different "national" deities, but He was the one and only universal God. Thus, after the Babylonian exile, the Israelites developed a new, much deeper, and more universalistic awareness of monotheism. Furthermore, it is worth pointing out that the roots of the Babylonian Jewish community were very ancient, and that, as it grew and prospered, that community tended to emphasize its antiquity. By the time it had produced its own version of the Talmud, it articulated a kind of local patriotism, highlighting that Abraham, the Father of the Nation, was born "beyond the river" (Euphrates), and that Euphrates and Tigris were the two rivers which flowed out of Eden according to Genesis 2:14. Thus, the Jews of Babylonia considered themselves the aristocracy of the Jewish people, and, in their eyes, the land of Mesopotamia acquired an aura of sanctity, second to the land of Israel, of course, but holier than any other country.

In the fifth century A.D., Philostorgius, in his *Church History*, writing of the rebuilding of the Jerusalem Temple, refers to the discovery of a Vault, and this is the earliest framework of the Royal Arch legend. Additionally, in the fourteenth century, Nikephoros Kallistos Xanthopoulos (Latinized as Nicephorus Callistus Xanthopulus), in his *Historia Ecclesiastica*, refers to a similar legend. Moreover, there is Biblical evidence for the Holy Royal Arch legend's reference to finding "part of the long-lost Sacred Law." In particular, in 2 Kings, chapter 22, and in 2 Chronicles, chapter 34, we find references to the priest Hilkiah discovering a law book during the execution of repair work in the Temple of Jerusalem. Biblical commentators commonly identify the previous book that was found by Hilkiah with the kernel of the Deuteronomy, and, in fact, this is the source of the original Irish Royal Arch legend.

The Masonic tale of Hiram Abiff is an attempt by the Rev. Dr. John Theophilus Desaguliers and by the Rev. James Anderson, another prominent Freemason and Protestant clergyman, to merge the Biblical narratives about Hiram Abiff and the stories of old Masonic manuscripts that refer to Noah and Bezalel, seeking thus to endow the Grand Lodge of London and Westminster with a distinctive Masonic identity, especially because, in those years, the Grand Lodge of London and Westminster was competing intensely with the Jacobites' Freemasonic forces. In February 1723, with the help of the Rev. Dr. John Theophilus Desaguliers, the

Rev. James Anderson, a Scottish Presbyterian clergyman, compiled the *Book of Constitutions of the Free-Masons* (also known among Freemasons as *Anderson's Constitutions*), reflecting the ethos and the Masonic strategy of such prominent players in the politics of the Grand Lodge of London and Westminster as the two noble Grand Masters, the Duke of Montagu (in 1721) and the Duke of Wharton (in 1723), and the Deputy Grand Master at the time of the publication of the *Constitutions*, the Rev. Dr. John Theophilus Desaguliers.

In addition, the very eminent Scottish author, editor, and Freemason William Preston, in his book entitled *Illustrations of Masonry,* originally published in 1772, highlights the significance of the two magnificent pillars that were erected at the porchway or entrance of the Temple at Jerusalem, which was completed by King Solomon. Those Pillars were made of molten brass, and the superintendent of the casting was Hiram Abiff. That on the left was called Boaz, which denotes *in strength*; that one the right Jachin, which denotes *to establish*; and when conjoined, they denote *stability*. Therefore, according to the rituals of the United Grand Lodge of England, the Grand Lodge of Scotland, and the Grand Lodge of Ireland, the pillar that stands on the north side of the door of a Masonic Lodge is called Boaz, and the pillar that stands on the south side of the door of a Masonic Lodge is called Jachin.

The eighteenth century was a period of political and religious ferment in England, and, therefore, the Grand Lodge of London and Westminster could not develop peacefully. In the years around 1740, there was a large number of Irish Freemasons in London, many of whom had been initiated into the Craft in Ireland. Many of those Irish Freemasons encountered difficulties in gaining entrance into London Lodges operating under the auspices of the Grand Lodge of London and Westminster. Therefore, in 1751, a group of those Irish Freemasons together with other Jacobite Freemasons founded a new Grand Lodge in London. According to their arguments, the Premier Grand Lodge had made innovations and had departed from "the landmarks," whereas they were practicing Freemasonry "according to the old institutions granted by Prince Edwin at York in A.D. 926." For this reason, they became known as the Ancients' Grand Lodge, and they were referring to their older rival, namely, the Grand Lodge of 1717, as "Moderns." In their Masonic certificates, issued to new members, the Ancients called themselves the "Grand Lodge of Free and Accepted

Masons of England according to the Old Constitutions." The book of constitutions of the Ancients' Grand Lodge of England was written by Laurence Dermott, a distinguished Irish merchant, and its title was *Ahiman Rezon*. The first edition of the *Ahiman Rezon* was published in 1756; a second one was published in 1764. It has often been said that the title *Ahiman Rezon* is derived from the Hebrew language and variously means "to help a brother," "will of selected brethren," "the secrets of prepared brethren," "royal builders," and "Brother Secretary"; the reason why Laurence Dermott used it and its meaning to him remain unclear.

The Ancients' Grand Lodge was oriented towards a more esoteric approach to Freemasonry, it was politically leaning towards the Tory Party, and it was associated with the Jacobites' secret attempts to restore King James VII (of Scotland) and II (of England) and his heirs to the British throne. Although the Jacobite Rising of 1715 ended in defeat, many Freemasons continued to support the Stuart dynasty. The Hanoverian King George I and, generally, the supporters of the Hanoverian dynasty were concerned about the Jacobites' influence on London Freemasonry, which was a secret organization meeting in small cabals, called Lodges, in the upper floors over inns, pubs, and coffee-houses around London. Thus, the supporters of the Hanoverian dynasty and the Whigs decided to reorganize, reform, and control Freemasonry. For this reason, the Grand Lodge of London and Westminster, which was founded in 1717, forbade all political and religious discussions within its Lodges, and it supported the House of Hanover. In addition, in its formative years, the Grand Lodge of London and Westminster, that is, the Moderns' Grand Lodge, methodically cultivated and promoted the highly controversial opinion that the Craft's history officially began in 1717, and it suppressed information pertaining to the history and the ethos of other Freemasonic entities.

In short, the Moderns' Grand Lodge, namely, the Grand Lodge of London and Westminster, represented the ethos of the rising bourgeoisie, modern capitalism, Protestant ethics as it has been analyzed by the great sociologist Max Weber, and an attempt to achieve an efficient historical compromise between the old nobility and the bourgeoisie, whereas the Ancients' Grand Lodge represented the ethos of the traditional feudal nobility, and it promoted a type of idealism that underestimated the needs of the new capitalist system. Finally, on 27 December 1813, the day of St. John the Evangelist, the Moderns' Grand Lodge of England and the

Ancients' Grand Lodge of England were amalgamated into the United Grand Lodge of England (UGLE), with the Duke of Sussex, who was the younger son of King George III and a Whig, as Grand Master. By the time of the Union, a considerable amount of revision had taken place in the ritual, and, in this context, the form of Freemasonry that was developed by the Moderns' Grand Lodge prevailed over the form of Freemasonry that was developed by the Ancients' Grand Lodge, and the United Grand Lodge of England changed the underpinning strategic vision of Freemasonry from being Christian and nobility-oriented to that of Non-Christian and bourgeois-oriented.

Nevertheless, the Ritual of the United Grand Lodge of England was taken from the Bible. Following the Union in 1813, a "Lodge of Reconciliation" was formed to reconcile the rituals worked under the two former Grand Lodges. In 1823, an "Emulation Lodge of Improvement" was established (under the sanction of the Lodge of Hope No. 7), teaching the ritual settled by the Lodge of Reconciliation, known as the Emulation Ritual. According to the Emulation Ritual, the First Degree takes place on the ground floor of King Solomon's Temple, the Second Degree takes place in the Middle Chamber of King Solomon's Temple, and the Third Degree takes place at the Porchway or Entrance of the Holy of Holies of King Solomon's Temple to symbolically describe a spiritual itinerary in Biblical terms. Moreover, the Emulation Ritual includes several religious invocations, prayers, and oaths. Thus, the Emulation Ritual is a religious ritual, as several Fathers of the Roman Catholic Church, including Pope Clement XII, Pope Pius VII, Pope Pius IX, and Pope Leo XIII, have justly pointed out. In fact, the Emulation Ritual, with its religious references, practices, and requirements, conflicts with the "Declaration" issued on 21 June 1985 by the United Grand Lodge of England, entitled "Freemasonry and Religion," which states in no uncertain terms that Freemasonry is not a religion. If the "regularity" of Symbolic Masonry is assumed to be necessarily dependent upon the use of religious Masonic rituals, then Symbolic Masonry should be directly overseen by the Church, like medieval Operative Masonry, unless one maintains that Freemasonry should develop and promote an alternative religious proposal of its own.

The form of Freemasonry that prevailed in the United Grand Lodge of England in the early nineteenth century became the prevailing form of Freemasonry throughout the British Isles, and, gradually, expanded throughout the world. For the Grand Lodges of England, Ireland, and Scotland, the aforementioned form of Freemasonry is the epitome of "Masonic regularity," and, in 1929, these three Grand Lodges, acting as the supreme "Guarantors" of what they have defined as "regular Freemasonry," formulated the basic principles for Grand Lodge recognition. According to the statement of the basic principles for Grand Lodge recognition that was drawn up in 1929 by the United Grand Lodge of England, the Grand Lodge of Scotland, and the Grand Lodge of Ireland, a Masonic Grand Lodge is "regular" if the following conditions are met: firstly, it has been established lawfully by a Grand Lodge that is duly recognized by the aforementioned three British Grand Lodges or it has been established lawfully by three or more Lodges that have been constituted according to the aforementioned three British Grand Lodges' rules of regularity; secondly, a belief in the Supreme Being, referred to as the Great Architect of the Universe, and His revealed will are essential preconditions for membership; thirdly, all initiates must take their obligations on or in full view of the Volume of the Sacred Law, namely, the major "Holy Book" of each one's religion, such as the Bible for Christians, the Torah for Jews, and the Quran for Muslims; fourthly, the membership of the Grand Lodge and individual Lodges must be exclusively of men, and Masonic regularity precludes any Masonic intercourse with mixed Masonic institutions, which admit women to membership; fifthly, the Grand Lodge must have sovereign jurisdiction over the Lodges that it controls, and international regular Freemasonry should be organized as a network of independent, territorially restricted, national Grand Lodges that are duly recognized by each other; sixthly, the three Great Lights of Freemasonry, namely, the Volume of the Sacred Law, the Square, and the Pair of Compasses, must be exhibited when the Grand Lodge or its subordinate Lodges are at work, and the chief of the Great Lights of Freemasonry is the Volume of the Sacred Law, namely, a religious book; seventhly, the discussion of religion and politics within the Lodge must be strictly prohibited; and, eighthly, the principles of the English Masons' "Ancient Landmarks," customs, and usages must be strictly observed.

The Rituals of the United Grand Lodge of England, the Grand Lodge of Scotland, and the Grand Lodge of Ireland are based on the aforementioned didactic tale of Hiram Abiff and on the use of King Solomon's Temple as the main symbol of architecture. At this point, it is important to highlight the difference between the concept of a myth and the concept of a tale. A "myth" is a traditional symbolic narrative whose purpose is to disclose the spiritual core of beings and things, and it is associated with the religious beliefs and, in general, with traditional cultural underpinnings of a human community, for which reason the historical origin of many myths is unknown. On the other hand, a "tale" is an imaginary narrative of an event, and it functions as a substitute for the lack of a genuine myth and a systematic philosophy. In particular, the tale of Hiram Abiff was adopted by the Moderns' Grand Lodge as a means of changing the mythological underpinnings of traditional societies in general and of traditional Masonic Lodges in particular and, thus, promoting the ethos of the Hanoverian dynasty and the Whig Party. Moreover, we must not lose sight of the fact that English Freemasonry has often functioned as a tool for cultural diplomacy in the service of British governments' foreign and domestic policy.

The origins of modern liberalism, of which the Whig Party is an integral part, can be seen most clearly in the thinking and politics linked to the English Revolution of 1688, namely, in British empiricism and constitutionalism. The principles of constitutionalism, religious tolerance, and commercial activity, which were promoted by the English Revolution of 1688, became a standard for European and American liberals in the eighteenth century. The successful American revolutionaries of the last quarter of the eighteenth century were attracted to John Locke's political philosophy, which was seen as the most important intellectual underpinning of the English Revolution of 1688. The motives and the results of the French Revolution of 1789 were more mixed, but, in rhetoric and institution, the French Revolution of 1789 was a liberal revolution, in the sense that it proclaimed the liberty of the individual, promoted respect for the right to private property as a means of eliminating the outrageous prerogatives of the feudal elites, and it praised the "self-made" humans. However, the end of the Napoleonic era left Europe dominated by monarchies and by the spirit of restoration, which maintained dark memories of and strong fears about previous revolutions, political disputes, and turmoil. In the aftermath of the Napoleonic era, conservatism, of which the Tory Party is an integral part, was articulated as a systematic and organized political expression of the advocates of tradition, historical continuity, and the preeminence of the institutions and the principles of the past.

In general, the transition from feudalism to capitalism marks an important historical progress. Feudalism, the dominant system in medieval Europe, was a system characterized by rigid social stratification, according to which everyone had a rigidly instituted position within an "organic whole," whose major constituent components were the class of the feudal lords, the class of the serfs, and the Church, whose major social role was to maintain a balance between the feudal lords and the serfs through religion. By the late Middle Ages, the bourgeois class, namely, a social class of professionals who were neither feudal lords nor serfs, deprecated the political, economic, and spiritual despotism of the feudal system, it revolted against feudalism, and it proclaimed that the social position of an individual should not be determined by feudal institutions, but it should be freely determined by individual action and by the interaction between individuals in the context of a free and fair society. One of the most characteristic examples of a bourgeois revolution in the modern era is the French Revolution of 1789, whose major motto was "Liberty, Equality, Fraternity."

However, the elite of the bourgeois class envisaged and instituted capitalism as the embodiment of human freedom in the domain of economics, and, for this reason, after the displacement of feudalism by capitalism, the liberty and the rights of the human individual were gradually largely displaced by and subordinated to the liberty and the rights of the capital itself and the capitalist elite. By the middle of the nineteenth century, the European peoples realized that capitalism had displaced feudalism, but, instead of ushering in liberty, equality, and fraternity among the people, capitalism tends to replace the authoritarian and exploitative relationship between the feudal lords and the serfs with a new authoritarian and exploitative relationship, namely, that between the capitalist class and the proletariat, that is, the working-class.

Even though capitalism is characterized by a significantly higher level of freedom in comparison with feudalism and has produced unprecedented economic wealth, it tends to substitute old contradictions with new ones and to substitute the "Kantian subject" with the "homo economicus." Therefore, socialism emerged as a criticism of and a revolt against capitalism, just as the bourgeois ideology had previously emerged as a criticism of and a revolt against feudalism. In fact, the term "socialism" first appeared in 1832 in *Le Globe*, a liberal French newspaper of the French philosopher and political economist Pierre Leroux, and, by the 1840s, socialism had already become the object of rigorous social-scientific analysis by the German economist and sociologist Lorenz von Stein. Moreover, in the nineteenth century, the English socialist intellectual and activist Thomas Hodgskin articulated a thorough critical analysis of capitalism and of the labor class under capitalism, and his writings exerted a significant influence on subsequent generations of socialists, including Karl Marx. In particular, from the perspective of Thomas Hodgskin, socialism implies an attempt to create a free and fair market, in the context of which production and exchange are based on the labor theory of value, freed from exploitative institutions, as part of natural right, which endows moral consciousness, the freedom of the individual, social justice, and social autonomy with ontological underpinnings in accordance with Thomas Hodgskin's deism.

Furthermore, in the twentieth century, the rapid globalization of the international economy (especially in the areas of production and finance) and the changing nature of the interstate system in the post-Cold War era contribute to the emergence of a "global," as opposed to "international," political economy. Global political economy refers to an economic space that transcends all country borders, while co-existing with an international economy that is based on transactions across country borders and is regulated by inter-state agreements and practices. Thus, global political economy identifies three different levels of economic space, specifically, supra-regional, national, and sub-regional. In addition, global political economy identifies at least three different levels of social organization, specifically, social forces, states (that is, national societies), and global society.

Intimately related to the issue of globalization is the issue of global governance. Global governance concerns the identification and management of those issues which necessarily affect every part of the globe. For instance, the globalization of the international political economy and its management, the global ramifications of a nuclear war, environmental questions and ecological concerns, technological advances, outer space affairs, global health issues, intercivilizational relations and intercultural communication, as well as the interplay between the notion of national self-interest and international common goods are issues of global governance.

In the eighteenth century, our British Freemasonic forebears had the brilliant idea of developing Symbolic Masonry from Operative Masonry, thus creating a fraternity whose declared goal is to build a better human being within a better society. In the eighteenth and the nineteenth centuries, the rituals and the constitutions of the British Freemasonries had their usefulness, their value, and, to some extent, their grandeur. But, in view of the historical and sociological remarks and arguments that I have hitherto put forward, one can rightly claim that, if a Freemasonic institution is fixated on the statement of the basic principles for Grand Lodge recognition that was drawn up in 1929 by the United Grand Lodge of England, the Grand Lodge of Scotland, and the Grand Lodge of Ireland, and if it focuses on rituals and catechisms that are founded on didactic tales inspired by the Bible or other religious books and on the ethos and the needs of the elites that ruled the United Kingdom during the Georgian and the Victorian eras, then it ultimately becomes a case of atavism, obsolete, and unable to provide highly cultured persons with anything culturally significant and intellectually fascinating. Such a Freemasonic institution is mainly suitable for the management and, more specifically, the manipulation of the "popolo" through glamour, networking, and vainglory. In fact, already in 1872, the distinguished and highly influential English Freemason and author John Yarker, in his book entitled *Notes on the Scientific and Religious Mysteries of Antiquity*, pages 157 to 158, argued that, "as the Masonic fraternity is now governed, the Craft is fast becoming the paradise of the *bon vivant*; of the 'charitable' hypocrite ... the manufacturer of paltry Masonic tinsel; the rascally merchant ... and the masonic 'Emperors' and other charlatans," and he proposed "the appointment of a higher (not pecuniary) standard of membership and morality, with exclusion from the 'purple' of all who inculcate frauds, sham, historical degrees, and other immoral abuses."

The Modern and Perfecting Rite of Symbolic Masonry seeks to rectify the above situation and enrich and ameliorate the system of Symbolic Masonry, often referred to as the "Craft," without, however, instituting or recognizing Masonic rites and degrees beyond the Craft. By "Masonic rites and degrees beyond the Craft," I mean a host of Masonic rites and degrees that were fabricated during the period from 1740 to 1800, mainly in the European Continent, by those Freemasons to whom the form of Freemasonry that is inspired by Operative Masonry was not sufficient, and who devised ceremonies that enlarged and expanded the scope of the established Masonic domain to encompass symbolic chivalric degrees usually inspired by the medieval Crusading Orders, degrees inspired by Rosicrucianism, and several other elaborations characterized by a high level of mysticism. Of the degrees that appeared, many were credited by various European and American Freemasons with a Scottish title and/or origin – even though none was literally connected to Scotland – and they included various legends and symbols related to the medieval Knights Templar.

Moreover, the development of several Masonic Rites and degrees is inextricably linked to social developments and political affairs. For instance, King James I of England and VI of Scotland used Masonry in order to consolidate his rule; King James II of England and VII of Scotland, who was deposed in the Glorious Revolution of 1688, and the Chevalier Ramsay used Scottish Rite Masonry, in particular, as a means of restoring the Stuart monarchy in the kingdoms of England, Scotland, and Ireland; Oliver Cromwell and radical parliamentarians used Masonry in order to unify and invigorate the social forces that opposed the Stuart Dynasty and in order to promote a Protestant capitalist elite; and King George I of Great Britain used the Grand Lodge of London and Westminster in order to consolidate the rule of the Hanoverian Dynasty, to which he belonged, and in order to promote a system of liberal oligarchy under his scepter.

Junior Overseer (J.O.): By the 1740s, in Avignon, the capital of the department of Vaucluse, there already existed several centers of Hermetic studies, often working in the context of Freemasonry and practicing the three Craft degrees and other higher "Scottish" degrees. One of the most influential members of the Hermetic community of Avignon was Dom Antoine-Joseph Pernety, who was a Benedictine and librarian of Frederick the Great of Prussia and the author of the *Dictionnaire Mytho-Hermétique* (1758). There is an important intellectual link between the Scottish Rite of Freemasonry and the Société des Illuminés d'Avignon (Society of the Illuminati of Avignon), which was founded in 1786 by Dom Antoine-Joseph Pernety and a Polish Count called Tadeusz Leszczyc-Grabianka. The Société des Illuminés d'Avignon was derived from an esoteric society that existed in Berlin prior to 1779, when Pernety joined it, and it was organized in two classes superior to Symbolic Masonry: the Novices or Minors, and the Illuminés (Illuminated); their head was called Magus and Pontiff. Moreover, the "Illuminés d'Avignon" were influenced by German Templar and Scottish Masonic degrees and legends related to Baron von Hund's "Rite of Strict Observance" and to the "Chevaliers Bienfaisants de la Cité Sainte" (Knights Beneficent of the Holy City) in Lyons. In 1783,

Pernety left Berlin, and he took up residence at a house he called Château Mont Thabor near Avignon provided by one of his disciples, the Marquis de Vaucroze. There, Pernety set up a lodge room for those who came to be known as the Illuminés d'Avignon. Among the Illuminés d'Avignon were the Duchess of Württemberg and Baron Erik Magnus Staël von Holstein, who was Chamberlain to Queen Sophia Magdalena of Sweden (the spouse of King Gustav III), and, in 1783, he was appointed chargé d'affaires to the Court of France, while, in 1785, he was named Ambassador of Sweden to France.

In the second half of the eighteenth century, several new Masonic and quasi-Masonic Orders and Rites were formed in France, such as the Ellus Coens, the Illuminés du Zodiaque, the Frères noirs, etc. In the 1760s, a French Freemasonic fraternity called the "Mother Lodge of Comtat-Venaissin" (in French, "Mère Loge du Comtat-Venaissin") was already working six degrees beyond the three Craft degrees. However, in 1775, the "Mother Lodge of Comtat-Venaissin" was suppressed by the Roman Catholic Inquisition.

In the 1770s, the chief seat of Scottish Masonry in Paris was the "Social Contract" Lodge (in French, "Le Contrat Social"), originally called the "Saint Lazarus" Lodge, which was working according to a "Philosophical Scottish Rite" (in French, "Rite Ecossais Philosophique") founded by the French physician and Hermeticist Dr. Boileau, who was a member of the Hermetic Rite of Avignon and a student of Pernety, under the auspices of the Grand Lodge of France. In 1766, the "Mother Lodge of Comtat-Venaissin" amalgamated with the "Social Contract" Lodge. Thus, after its suppression in Avignon by the Roman Catholic Inquisition, the "Mother Lodge of Comtat-Venaissin" was revived in the bosom of the "Social Contract" Lodge in Paris under the auspices of the English-style Grand Lodge of France and, subsequently, under the auspices of the Grand Orient of France, which is a purely French Masonic institution officially formed in 1773 and representing a French reformation of traditional English Freemasonry.

According to the English "Grand Lodge" system, the Grand Lodge of Symbolic Masonry is not only autonomous vis-à-vis the administrative authorities of the various Bodies of "higher degrees" (namely, vis-à-vis Masonic Orders beyond the Craft), but the latter depend on the Grand Lodge's approval of their operation, since the Grand Lodge of Symbolic Masonry has the exclusive authority to award the degree of a Master Mason, which is a necessary qualification for continuing one's Masonic journey beyond the three Craft Degrees. On the other hand, according to the French "Grand Orient" system, the supreme administrative authority of the "higher degrees," specifically, the Supreme Council of the 33rd Degree of the Ancient and Accepted Scottish Rite, governs Symbolic Masonry, too, thus maintaining full authority over the Degrees 1°–33°.

The thirty-three degrees of the Ancient and Accepted Scottish Rite (A.A.S.R.) are the following: (1°) Entered Apprentice, (2°) Fellow Craft, (3°) Master Mason, (4°) Secret Master, (5°) Perfect Master, (6°) Intimate Secretary, (7°) Provost and Judge, (8°) Intendant of the Buildings, (9°) Elect of Nine, (10°) Elect of Fifteen, (11°) Sublime Elect, (12°) Grand Master Architect, (13°) Royal Arch of Enoch, (14°) Scotch Knight of Perfection (or Grand Elect Perfect and Sublime Mason), (15°) Knight of the East or of the Sword, (16°) Prince of Jerusalem, (17°) Knight of the East and West, (18°) Knight of the Pelican and Eagle and Sovereign Prince Rose Croix of Heredom, (19°) Grand Pontiff, (20°) Venerable Grand Master of the Symbolic Lodges, or Master ad Vitam, (21°) Patriarch Noachite or Prussian Knight, (22°) Prince of Libanus, (23°) Chief of the Tabernacle, (24°) Prince of the Tabernacle, (25°) Knight of the Brazen Serpent, (26°) Prince of Mercy, (27°) Commander of the Temple, (28°) Knight of the Sun, (29°) Knight of Saint Andrew, (30°) Grand Elected Knight Kadosh or Knight of the Black and White Eagle, (31°) Grand Inspector Inquisitor Commander, (32°) Sublime Prince of the Royal Secret, and (33°) Sovereign Grand Inspector General. Many of these degrees are conferred by name only; and the major initiatory degrees of the A.A.S.R. that are always worked in full are the 18th degree and the 30th degree. The 30th degree of the Ancient and Accepted Scottish Rite (A.A.S.R.), which is called Grand Elected Knight Kadosh, is the supreme initiatory degree of the A.A.S.R., and, in Hebrew, "Kadosh" means holy or consecrated. The 31st degree, the 32nd degree, and the 33rd degree are administrative, roughly corresponding to the judiciary, the legislature, and the executive.

The characteristic jewel of the 33rd degree rests upon a Cross Potent: it is a nine-pointed star, namely, one formed by three triangles of gold one upon the other, and interlaced; from the lower part of the left side to the upper part of the right, a sword extends, and in the opposite direction is a hand of (as it is called) *justice*; in the center is a crowned double-headed eagle, holding a naked sword in its claws, and having, on the right-hand side, a balance and, on the left-hand side, a pair of compasses united with a square; around the eagle, runs a band bearing the Latin inscriptions *"Ordo ab Chao"* (meaning *Order out of Chaos) and "Deus Meumque Jus" (meaning God and My Right)*; the band is enclosed by two circles formed by two serpents, each biting its own tail; of the smaller triangles that are formed by the intersection of the greater ones, those nine that are nearest the band are of crimson color, and each of them has one of the letters that compose the word *S.A.P.I.E.N.T.I.A., that is, Wisdom.*

In 1754, in the College of Jesuits at Clermont outside Paris, the Chevalier de Bonneville established the Chapter of Clermont, honoring the Duc de Clermont, then Grand Master of the English-style Grand Lodge of France. The Chapter of Clermont may have worked as many as twenty-five degrees, known as the "higher degrees," the highest of which was called Sublime Prince of the Royal Secret. This Masonic organization was an asylum of the adherents of the Stuart cause, most of whom were Scotsmen. One of those "higher degrees" was known as Scottish Master, hence the origin of the name Scottish Rite. In 1758, the aforementioned degrees were introduced into Germany by the Marquis Gabriel de Lernay, a French officer captured during the Seven Years' War; he established a military Lodge in Berlin with the help of two Germans: the Baron de Printzen, a Mason who was Master of the "Three Globes" Mother Lodge at Berlin, and Philipp Samuel Rosa, a disgraced former pastor. Thus, in 1758, these degrees were adopted by the Grand Lodge of the Three Globes, also known as Grand National Mother Lodge of the Prussian States. In the same year, these degrees were revived in Paris under the auspices of a Masonic Order that was called the Council of Emperors of East and West. However, in consequence of internal warfare in the Council of Emperors of East and West, which was arguably caused by Jesuits, who endeavored to sow dissension with the view of suppressing this newly-established Masonic Order, a new Masonic organization was formed which was called the Council of Knights of the East. The Council of Knights of the East practiced what was known as the Rite of Perfection, the name by which the twenty-five Clermont Degrees were originally known. The Council of Knights of the East was representing mainly the bourgeoisie and, generally, the middle class as well as the Whig ideology, whereas the Council of Emperors of East and West was representing mainly the nobility and the old conservative ideology.

In 1761, the Council of Emperors of East and West managed to defeat the Council of Knights of the East and assume exclusive regular control over the Rite of Perfection, and it granted a patent to a merchant called Stephen Morin to propagate the Rite of Perfection, and installed him as a Grand Inspector of the Rite of Perfection. According to Albert Mackey's *Encyclopedia of Freemasonry*, most probably, Stephen Morin was a member of a French-American Huguenot family. The original of the aforementioned document has not been found, but Freemasons know about it only from the copy preserved in the *Golden Book* of the Comte de Grasse-Tilly, founder of the Supreme Council of the Ancient and Accepted Scottish Rite for France. In 1761, Morin arrived in San Domingo, where he started propagating the Rite of Perfection, and, by virtue of his patent, he appointed many Inspectors for both the West Indies and the United States of America.

Morin was by no means the proper person to act as the Grand Inspector and chief propagator of the Rite of Perfection in America, because his philosophical and Masonic education was poor, and he made wrong decisions with regard to the choice of his lieutenants. In particular, he appointed several merchants of dubious morality and rather bad reputation, even members of the American-Jewish underworld, as his lieutenants. Thus, unworthy, or at least underqualified, persons played an instrumental role in the history of the Rite of Perfection in America for approximately the next forty years.

Sometime between 1763 and 1767, Morin appointed Henry Andrew Francken, a naturalized French citizen of Dutch origin, then resident of Jamaica and employed as a customs officer, "Deputy Inspector General of all the Superior Degrees of Free and Accepted Masons in West Indies." Henry Andrew Francken played an important role in the formation and propagation of the Rite of Perfection in the American colonies. In 1768, having previously settled in New York, where he was appointed court interpreter, Henry Andrew Francken formed the so-called Ineffable Lodge of Perfection at Albany, New York, and he appointed Moses Michael Hays (a Jewish businessman who later became very wealthy) Deputy Inspector and Knight Kadosh with the power to constitute Grand Chapters of Knights of the Sun and of Kadosh in West Indies and North America. Moreover, Henry Andrew Francken wrote several ritual books. In 1781, Hays made eight Deputy Inspectors, four of whom were later important in the establishment of the first Supreme Council of the Ancient and Accepted Scottish Rite in South Carolina, namely: Isaac da Costa (a distinguished Jewish merchant and shipping agent) Deputy Inspector for South Carolina, Abraham Forst Deputy Inspector for Virginia, Joseph M. Myers Deputy Inspector for Maryland, and Barend M. Spitzer Deputy Inspector for Georgia. In February 1783, Da Costa went to Charleston, South Carolina, where he established the "Sublime Grand Lodge of Perfection."

After Da Costa's death, in November 1783, Hays appointed Myers as Da Costa's successor. In 1788, joined at Charleston by Forst and Spitzer, Myers opened a Grand Council of Princes of Jerusalem claiming jurisdiction over Lodges of Perfection. Moreover, Myers and his Masonic associates fabricated additional high-degree bodies, beyond the Rite of Perfection. Thus, in 1801, the ruling bodies of the Rite of Perfection in South Carolina, which were originally established by Da Costa in 1783, became the Supreme Council of the so-called Ancient and Accepted Scottish Rite (A.A.S.R.) for the Southern Jurisdiction, which had the authority to confer thirty-three degrees, most of which existed in parts of previous high-degree systems. The formation of the "Mother" Supreme Council of the A.A.S.R. in Charleston took place in May 1801.

During the aforementioned obscure, formative period of the American Lodges of the Rite of Perfection and of the A.A.S.R., there emerged a peculiar Masonic legend, according to which Frederick the Great, King of Prussia, was the Supreme Head of the Rite of Perfection. Additionally, according to the same legend, Frederick the Great, on his death-bed, ratified the Grand Constitutions of 1786, which underpin the structure and the operation of the Ancient and Accepted Scottish Rite (A.A.S.R.), and he personally instituted the 33rd Degree of the A.A.S.R., delegating his powers as a Sovereign of Masonry to local Supreme Councils, each one of which would govern the A.A.S.R. in its jurisdiction. The original Grand Constitutions of Scottish Masonry had been written in French, but, in 1834, a Latin version of them alleged to have been signed by Frederick the Great was accepted as genuine by the Supreme Council of the A.A.S.R. for France; however, this document is a forgery. The previous legend, according to which Frederick the Great was the Supreme Head of the Rite of Perfection, the author of the Grand Constitutions of 1786, and the creator of the 33rd Degree of the A.A.S.R., was, most probably, fabricated by founding Grand Inspectors of the Rite of Perfection in America in order to increase the commercial value of the Rite's degrees and as a marketing tool for the promotion of the 33rd Degree of the A.A.S.R.

The truth is that Frederick the Great was never actively involved in the Rite of Perfection, and that he neither ratified the Grand Constitutions of 1786, which have been, falsely, attributed to him, nor did he institute the 33rd Degree of the A.A.S.R. Nevertheless, the Grand Constitutions of 1786 constitute the fundamental law of the A.A.S.R. in every Supreme Council that has been regularly derived from the Charleston Supreme Council (known as the "Mother Supreme Council of the world"), and Albert Pike, who was the Sovereign Grand Commander of the Southern Jurisdiction of the A.A.S.R. for the U.S.A. from 1859 until his death in 1891, believed that the Grand Constitutions of 1786 were authentic and had been ratified by Frederick the Great. On 19 December 1861, the Grand Lodge of the Three Globes in Berlin published a Protocol, in which it officially stated the following:

> Frederick the Great is said to have revised, reorganized, and increased from 25 to 33 degrees the system of High Degrees in a Supreme Council held in Berlin.... With regard to this subject, Bro. Le Blanc de Marconnay sent a letter dated 25 May 1833 from New York to the Directory of the Grand National Mother Lodge of the Three Globes.... Are these historical traditions founded on truth? ... The answer that the Directory returned, on 17 August 1833, says: "The Grand National Mother Lodge of the Three Globes was founded on 13 September 1740, under the authority of Frederick the Great, who was its first Grand Master. He never had anything to do with the organization and legislation of the Grand Lodge. Anything that concerns his having, in 1786, originated a high Masonic Senate, etc., has no historical basis" ... [Georg Franz Burkhard] Kloss attends to this subject in a long examination in his *History of Freemasonry in France* and stamps the Constitutions and Statutes of the Ancient and Accepted Rite as "the grand lie of the Order." As harsh as this judgment may appear at a first glance, the Directory of the Grand Lodge of the Three Globes, after repeated researches in the archives and historical collections, cannot help sustaining it.

As I have already mentioned, the predominant form of the Scottish Rite was established in 1801 in Charleston, South Carolina. Colonel John Mitchell, a native of Ireland and an officer of the American Army in the

Revolutionary War, served as its first Sovereign Grand Commander. Between 1813 and 1815, the second Scottish Rite Supreme Council was organized in the northern part of the United States to counter a clandestine Scottish Rite Supreme Council that had been created by the French Freemason Joseph Cerneau in New York. In 1827, a territorial agreement was reached between the Northern and the Southern Jurisdictions designating the fifteen States north of the Mason–Dixon Line in east of the Mississippi River as the boundary line between the two Jurisdictions. The degrees 4th–33rd that the Scottish Rite superimposed on the three degrees of Symbolic Masonry are a system of didactic narratives, allegories, and symbols designated to help Master Masons perfect themselves as human beings and Freemasons.

After the formation of the "Mother" Supreme Council of the A.A.S.R. in Charleston, in May 1801, other Supreme Councils of the A.A.S.R. were formed internationally. The A.A.S.R. was introduced by Comte de Grasse-Tilly into France (1804); from France it passed into Italy (1805), Spain (1811), Belgium (1817), etc. In 1813, an officer from the Supreme Council at Charleston elevated several New York Masons to the 33rd degree of the A.A.S.R. and, thus, organized a Supreme Council of the A.A.S.R. for the "Northern Masonic District and Jurisdiction." The "Supreme Council, Scottish Rite, Northern Jurisdiction," based in Lexington, Massachusetts, oversees the Ancient and Accepted Scottish Rite in the following fifteen States: Connecticut, Delaware, Illinois, Indiana, Maine, Massachusetts, Michigan, New Jersey, New Hampshire, New York, Ohio, Pennsylvania, Rhode Island, Wisconsin, and Vermont; in every other State of the U.S.A., the Ancient and Accepted Scottish Rite is overseen by the "Supreme Council, Ancient and Accepted Scottish Rite, Southern Jurisdiction, U.S.A.," which is commonly known as the "Mother Supreme Council of the World," and, since 1911, it is based in Washington, D.C. Moreover, during the nineteenth century, additional Supreme Councils were established in the U.S.A. For instance, a separate Supreme Council was established in 1839 in New Orleans; the so-called King David Supreme Council, populated predominantly by colored men, was established in 1856; and the so-called United Supreme Council was formed in 1881 as a result of the amalgamation of previous Supreme Councils that were created and populated predominantly by men of African descent (including the King David Supreme Council).

In 1819, the aforementioned "Mother" Supreme Council of the A.A.S.R. in Charleston granted a Patent to the Duke of Sussex (the first Grand Master of the United Grand Lodge of England) to form a Supreme Council in England, but he failed to act upon it, probably due to his keen desire to see the UGLE maintain its "purist" policy, according to which pure Ancient Masonry consists only of the degrees of the Entered Apprentice, the Fellow Craft, and the Master Mason, including the Supreme Order of the Holy Royal Arch. Finally, the Supreme Council for England and Wales was founded in 1845, receiving its Patent from the aforementioned Northern Masonic Jurisdiction.

Orator: As the first three degrees of the A.A.S.R. correspond with Symbolic or Craft Masonry, they are no longer worked as part of the A.A.S.R. Different Supreme Councils around the world have revised the rituals of the A.A.S.R. according to each Supreme Council's particular mentality and Masonic culture. However, the spiritual core of all the degrees of the A.A.S.R. remains the same. Therefore, let me present to you the standard teachings and symbols of the thirty degrees that are worked as part of the A.A.S.R., namely, from the 4th degree to the 33rd degree:

The 4th to the 14th degrees constitute the Lodge of Perfection. Usually, these degrees are conferred all together in one ceremony or, alternatively, in parts, in two or three ceremonies.

The 4th degree teaches that the Secret Masters are partakers of the Holy Truth, and that they can convey their virtue only through devotion and service to the world, namely, through historical action. In particular, according to the symbolic teachings of the 4th degree, there was only one entrance to the Holy of Holies of the First Temple of Jerusalem, in the East, and it was called "Ziza," a Hebrew word meaning "brightness." Hence, the emblem of the 4th degree is a key on which the letter Z is engraved. According to the symbolic content of the 4th degree, the Freemason acquires the symbolic key with which one can open the door of Ziza and cross it, thus entering the realm of pure truth, symbolized by the Holy of Holies of the First Temple of Jerusalem, after one's soul has overcome the obstacles posed by passions, prejudices, and illusions. As is reasonable, the Password of the 4th degree is Ziza, and the Sacred Word of this degree is Yod, which is the tenth letter of the Hebrew alphabet, and, in the context of the Kabbalah, Yod is represented by a mere dot, which symbolizes a divine point of energy.

The 5th degree teaches that, for the Perfect Masters, age is not measured by units of time, but by deeds, and that the monument of the Work of a person who has worked hard, sincerely, and wisely shines and feeds him or her with the life force of the Creator. The 6th degree teaches that our duty is to act with the best intentions and to judge fairly and honestly. The 7th degree teaches that we have intellect, feelings, instincts, strength, abilities, and commitment, and that we cannot achieve anything significant with these qualities if they are not properly coordinated, that is, if they are not governed by a higher law, a higher principle. In his Republic, 443d–e, Plato argues that one has cured his soul if he has "attained to self-mastery and beautiful order within himself, and . . . harmonized these three principles [the three parts of the soul, namely, reason, the emotions, and the appetites] . . . linked and bound all three together and made himself a unit, one man instead of many, self-controlled and in unison." The 8th degree teaches that progress cannot be achieved without learning and improvement, that important endeavours can be carried out with the help of others, and that knowledge can be lost if not preserved and passed on to others.

The "Elect" degrees, namely, the 9th, the 10th, and the 11th degrees, recount the mode of the arrest and the punishment of the assassins of Hiram Abiff by special task forces organized by Solomon King of Israel. According to the didactic story of the 9th degree, a task force composed of nine Master Masons found one of the assassins of Hiram Abiff, and the most ardent of the nine killed him, severed the head from the body, and taking it in one hand and his dagger in the other, with the eight returned to Jerusalem. According to the didactic story of the 10th degree, fifteen Master Masons, among whom were the nine Master Masons mentioned in the 9th degree, found the other villains, seized them, and, binding them in chains, conducted them to Jerusalem, where they were sentenced to death and executed. According to the didactic story of the 11th degree, King Solomon instituted this degree, both as a recompense for the zeal and constancy of the Elect of Fifteen and in order to honor other deserving Masons, who excel in science and in social and moral virtues. In brief, the "Elect" degrees teach that arbitrary ambition, fanaticism, and social oppression should be overthrown and dispelled by the sword of justice and freedom, and that true and faithful Freemasons are earnest, honest, and sincere, and they protect the people against illegal impositions and exactions.

The 12th degree is alleged to have been established as a school of instruction for the more advanced Craftsmen in order to ensure uniformity in work and vigor in its prosecution, and to prepare Master Masons for promotion to the 13th degree, which is the main focal point of the Lodge of Perfection.

The 13th degree is devoted to the correct pronunciation of the name of the Absolute Being, the deity. According to the 13th degree, Enoch, an ancient Patriarch of knowledge and civilization prior to Noah's flood, had a divinely inspired vision in which he contemplated the Ineffable Name of God, specifically, the Holy Tetragrammaton, which consists of four Hebrew letters, namely, Yod–Heh–Vav–Heh (YHVH), and it corresponds to the Sefira of Chokhmah, whereas the Hebrew divine name that corresponds to the Sefira of Kether is Ehyeh, and the Hebrew divine name that corresponds to the Sefira of Binah is YHVH Elohim.

The Holy Tetragrammaton

Hebrew	Letter name
י	Yod
ה	Heh
ו	Vav
ה	Heh

Etymologists teach that the Holy Tetragrammaton, that is, the name "Yehovah" (or "Jehovah"), means "the One who I am"; and that explanation is in accordance with the Volume of the Sacred Law, which attributes the words "I am that I am" to God, as we read in the book of Exodus, 3:14. It is, in fact, the only name that we can give to the Absolute Being whenever we refer to the Absolute Being's essence, which is totally transcendent. In the case of the Absolute Being, the essence of being is identified with the presence of being. Additionally, according to the 13th degree, the Holy Tetragrammaton contains the following Trinitarian formula: by uniting Yod with the first Heh, we obtain a name of the deity that means Generator; by uniting the first Heh with the Vav, we obtain a name of the deity that means Creative Word; and, by uniting Vav with another Heh, a third divine name appears, which continues from the first and the second, so that, when they are all united in one Big Name, we can find Three in One. Those Masons who have studied and understood the aforementioned secrets are ultimately proclaimed Grand Elect Perfect and Sublime Masons, namely, they are awarded the 14th degree. Therefore, the Sacred Word of both the 13th and the 14th degrees is "Yehovah" (or "Jehovah").

The 15th to the 18th degrees constitute the Chapter of Rose Croix, and they are usually conferred all together in one ceremony. The 15th degree is devoted to the exercise of freedom, and its characteristic symbol is the acronym L.D.P., which stands for both "Liberté De Penser," meaning "freedom of thought," and "Liberté De Passer," meaning "freedom to pass." The 16th degree is focused on the reward due to bravery, constancy, and perseverance. The 17th degree reminds us of the amalgamation of different European nations in the context of the Order of the Knights of Malta during the Second Crusade. According to the 17th degree, Freemasonry conducts its own Crusades, which, in contrast to the medieval Crusades, are aimed at combating bigotry and superstition.

In the British world, the standard transactions of the A.A.S.R. are conducted in the 18th degree. The 18th degree teaches that the Rose symbolizes secrecy and silence as well as Him who is the "Rose of Sharon and the Lily of the Valley," since, in the Song of Solomon, we find a reference to the Savior under the mystical title of the "Rose of Sharon"; the cross represents the Cross of Calvary, red with the holy blood; the pelican symbolizes the Savior Jesus Christ who shed his blood for the salvation of humanity, and, therefore, it symbolizes Jesus Christ in his mediatorial character, while the eagle is a symbol of Jesus Christ in his divine character. According to the 18th degree Ritual, the Candidate is symbolically admitted in a Chapter of Princes Rose Croix of Heredom "at the ninth hour of the day," when the earth quakes, the rocks are rent, the veil of the Temple is rent in twain, and darkness overspreads the earth, highlighting the Passion Narrative in Matthew's Gospel (27:50–51).

The 18th degree refers to the figurative passage of man through the depths of darkness and the Valley of the Shadow of Death to the Mansions of Light, accompanied and sustained by the three theological virtues, namely, Faith, Hope, and Charity, which are symbolically found by symbolically searching in and about the Pillars in the North, the South, and the West for the lost Word. Faith, corresponding to the North, supports the aspirant when tempted to despair; Hope, corresponding to the South, cheers the aspirant on his/her road; Charity, corresponding to the

West, sustains the aspirant in every trial, until, having travelled through the abyss of darkness, he/she arrives at the Mansions of Light, corresponding to the East. The 18th degree teaches that, assisted by these three virtues, the candidate will succeed in attaining the Rosicrucians' ultimate goal, which is that Word on which the eternal salvation of humanity depends. In this degree, the aspirant arrives at the Eastern part of the Lodge, where he/she discovers the Lost Word as Emmanuel, meaning "God with us." Thus, the Password of the 18th degree is Emmanuel, and the Sacred Word of the 18th degree is I.N.R.I., namely, the initials of the Latin sentence that was placed upon the Cross of Jesus Christ: "Jesus Nazarenus Rex Judaeorum" (as we read in Matthew 27:37, Mark 15:26, Luke 23:38, John 19:19–20). In fact, they used the letter I instead of the letter J because there was no letter J in the Roman, the Hebrew, and the Greek alphabets (and the letter J first came into use when the Gospel stories were translated into German). Moreover, the Rosicrucians interpret I.N.R.I. as the initials of the Hermetic (that is, alchemical) principles "Igne Natura Renovatur Integra" (meaning "by fire nature is perfectly renewed") and "Igne Nitrum Roris Invenitur" (meaning "by fire the nitre of the dew is discovered"), and as the initials of the Hebrew names of the ancient elements, namely: "Iaminim" (water), "Nour" (fire), "Ruach" (air), and "Iebschah" (earth).

The 19th to the 30th degrees constitute the Council of Kadosh. Usually, these degrees are conferred all together in one ceremony or, alternatively, in parts, in two or three ceremonies.

The major motto of the 19th and the 20th degrees is "Laus Deo," meaning "praise (be) to God." Pontiff means bridge-builder. The 19th degree, which is called Grand Pontiff, teaches that we must build bridges from one human being to another, serving the ideas of Justice, Truth, and Tolerance, and, thus, leading humanity to a state of good spirit, or happiness. The 20th degree, which is called Venerable Grand Master of the Symbolic Lodges, or Master ad Vitam, is devoted to the protection of the pure core of Symbolic Masonry. In particular, the 20th degree teaches that the main goal of Freemasonry is that of philosophy, namely, finding the truth and serving the idea of goodness; but, as the 20th degree explicitly points out, ignorance, ambition, ostentation, and false beliefs have veiled the truths of Freemasonry, and, frequently, new and fantastic Masonic degrees were invented and unimaginably lofty Masonic titles were handed out. Thus, the 20th degree boldly assigns Freemasons the responsibility to rid Freemasonry of deception, corruption, false narratives, and vanity.

The major motto of the 21st and the 22nd degrees is "Omnia Tempus Alit," meaning "all time feeds or crushes." The 21st degree teaches that we must judge fairly and impartially and not expect to gain benefits through a bad deed. The 22nd degree teaches that work is not an insult and a curse but a blessing, because it creates everything and, therefore, is a divine energy and the condition of every civilization.

The major motto of the 23rd, the 24th, and the 25th degrees is "Corde Gladioque Potens," meaning "powerful in heart and sword." The 23rd degree teaches that we should contemplate and approach the cause of being. The 24th degree teaches that we must follow the rules of correct reasoning, become free, and have a faith based on self-cultivation and self-confidence. The 25th degree teaches that we must free ourselves from the logic of material necessities. The Biblical story of the "brazen serpent," to which the 25th degree alludes, is recounted in Numbers 21:5–9.

The major motto of the 26th, the 27th, and the 28th degrees is "Ardens Gloria Surgit," meaning "burning glory rises." The 26th degree teaches altruism and good will. The 27th degree teaches struggle for the liberation of humanity, just as the Knights Templar fought for the liberation of the Holy Land. The 28th degree teaches that the Absolute Being, traditionally symbolized by the Sun, is transcendent, the essence of the Absolute Being is not accessible to the human intellect, reason is the supreme stage of mental development, and the principle of analogy, that is, thinking through analogies, is the key to understanding the logically inconceivable.

The major motto of the 29th and the 30th degrees is "Architectonis Magni Dei Gloria," meaning "glory to the Great Architect God." The 29th degree teaches humility, patience, self-sacrifice, love of neighbor, meekness, magnanimity, courage, honesty, truthfulness, and dignity. Virtue, Truth, and Honor are the three most essential qualities of a Knight of Saint Andrew. The Grand Lodge of Scotland recognizes Saint Andrew as the patron Saint of Scottish Freemasonry.

In the 30th degree of the Ancient and Accepted Scottish Rite (A.A.S.R.), the attention of the candidate is directed towards a mysterious ladder that has two supports and seven steps. The first support on the right bears the Hebrew name "Oheb Eloah," meaning "love of God," and the second support on the left bears the Hebrew name "Oheb Koerobo," meaning "love of one's neighbor." The seven ascending steps symbolize the hierarchy of the liberal sciences (namely, Grammar, Rhetoric, Logic, Arithmetic, Geometry, Music, and Astronomy), through which abstract thought and systematic knowledge of the universe become possible. The seven descending steps symbolize seven moral virtues, through which one can turn one's consciousness towards one's fellow-humans, "down here" (in this world), in order to promote humanity's prosperity and progress; these seven virtues bear the following Hebrew names: "Tseda-kah," which means justice and charity, "Schor Laban," which means white ox and, symbolically, goodness and innocence, "Mathok," which means gentleness and mildness, "Emounah," which means trust in truth, "Hamal Saghia," which means Great Work and emphasizes the moral significance of practical work, "Sabbal," which means burden and moral responsibility, and "Ghemoul Binah Thebounah," which means that prudence leads to wisdom. Furthermore, the ritual of the 30th degree is strongly Templar in tone, and, in this degree's ceremony, the candidate is pledged to honor the memory of Jacques de Molay, the last Grand Master of the Crusading Order of the Knights Templar, by punishing crime, by protecting innocence and people's rights, by opposing any type of mental and political despotism that undermines people's rational faculty and fundamental freedoms, and by fighting against oppression and injustice. Thus, the Password of the 30th degree is given as follows: one says "Menachem Nekam," meaning "comfort through vengeance," or "comfort through the punishment of the guilty," and the other replies by saying "Pharasch-Chol," meaning "all is explained," or "all is understood." Moreover, the Sacred Word of the 30th degree is "Nekam Adonai," meaning "Vengeance, My Lord."

It is noteworthy that the Scottish adherents of the exiled British King James II who followed him into exile (after the landing of the Prince of Orange in 1688) brought to the English Court at St. Germain (which had been placed at the disposal of James II by the French King Louis XIV) Scottish Masonic traditions intermingled with Templarism. The development of Scottish Masonry and of Masonic Templar degrees and legends in France was significantly boosted by the seminal *Ramsay's Oration*, written in 1737. The Chevalier Andrew Michael Ramsay was a native of Scotland, a Knight of the French Order of St. Lazarus, and, in 1724 and 1725, tutor to the two sons of the exiled James III ("The Old Pretender"), the son of Great Britain's exiled King James II. In fact, Ramsay was born in Ayr, Scotland, the son of a baker, he was educated at the University of Edinburgh, and, when King James II threw the mace into the Thames and fled to Paris, he went to the Netherlands, where he served with the English auxiliaries and studied mystical theology. Ramsay was attracted to the mysticism of quietism as practiced in the circle of George Garden, a Scottish Church minister and leading figure of the early Scottish Episcopal Church, at Rosehearty, in the historical county of Aberdeenshire in Scotland. In 1710, Ramsay travelled to Rijnsburg to meet Antoinette Bourignon de la Porte, a French-Flemish mystic and adventurer, and, afterwards, he also met Jeanne-Marie Bouvier de la Motte-Guyon, known simply as Mme Guyon, who was a prominent French mystic and advocate of quietism. Mme Guyon emphasized and taught meditation on love. In August 1710, Ramsay went on to stay with François Fénelon, a French Roman Catholic archbishop, mystical theologian, poet, writer, and preceptor of the grandsons of Louis XIV. Under Fénelon's influence, Ramsay was converted to Roman Catholicism. In January 1724, Ramsay was sent to Rome as tutor to James III's two sons, Charles Edward and Henry, and, in November 1724, Ramsay was back in Paris.

In 1737, in Paris, Ramsay delivered a thought-provoking and controversial Oration before the English Provincial Grand Lodge of France, of which he was Grand Chancellor and Orator. In his Oration, Ramsay argued that the founders of Freemasonry "were not simple workers in stone," but crusader knights "who vowed to restore the Temple" in the Holy Land, in imitation of the ancient Israelites, who, "while they handled the trowel and mortar with one hand, in the other, they held the sword and buckler." Thus, Ramsay attempted to integrate the institution and the ethos of medieval chivalry into Freemasonry and to cultivate mystical theology through legends about the cultural interaction between crusading knights, especially the Templars, and Eastern mystics during the Crusaders' expeditions in the Eastern Roman Empire and the Middle East.

In particular, according to the Chevalier Ramsay's aforementioned oration, at the time of the Crusades, many princes, lords, and knights associated themselves and vowed to restore the Christians' Temple in Jerusalem and to employ themselves in restoring the traditional form and glory of their architecture. Thus, they agreed upon several secret ancient signs and symbolic words drawn from the Christian religion in order to recognize themselves among the heathens and Saracens. Furthermore, according to the same oration, those secret signs and words were only communicated to those who promised solemnly never to divulge them. As a result, the Chevalier Ramsay maintains, the previous sacred promise, often associated with the Templars' inner circle, was not heretical, but instead it was a holy bond to unite Christians of all nationalities into one confraternity. Moreover, according to Ramsay, sometime afterwards, Masonry was somehow united with the Knights of St. John, and, from that time, the Masons' Lodges took the name of Lodges of St. John.

The "Poor Fellow-Soldiers of Christ and of the Temple of Solomon" (in Latin, *Pauperes Commilitones Christi Templique Solomonici*), commonly known as the "Knights Templar," the "Order of the Temple" (in French, *Ordre du Temple or Templiers*), or simply as "Templars," were among the most famous Crusading Orders. When the Holy Land was lost, support for the Order faded. Rumors about the Templars' secret initiation ceremony created mistrust, and King Philip IV of France, deeply in debt and jealous of the Templars' financial prosperity and power, took advantage of the situation. In 1307, many Templars in France were arrested, tortured into giving false confessions, and then burned at the stake. King Philip IV had Jacques de Molay, the 23rd and last Grand Master of the Knights Templar, burned at the stake in Paris, in March 1314. Moreover, under pressure from King Philip IV, Pope Clement V disbanded the Order in 1312. Since at least the eighteenth century, several Masonic Bodies have embraced Templar symbols and rituals, mainly using the historical Order of the Temple as a symbol in order to teach moral lessons emphasizing the significance of committing oneself to noble goals, fortitude, and the need for a humanistic crusade.

Both the aforementioned oration made by the Chevalier Ramsay in 1737 in Paris and the Rite of Strict Observance, which was set up in Germany in the 1760s by Baron von Hund, have propagated the following legend: after the destruction of the Templar Order and the execution of its last Grand Master, Jacques de Molay, a number of Knights Templar escaped, came together on the mysterious Mount Heredom near Kilwinning where, to avoid persecution, they turned themselves into Freemasons, and transferred the Templar secrets into the secrets of Freemasonry. However, this legend is historically unsubstantiated and should be treated as a tale for the following reasons: Firstly, the Knights Templar were never persecuted in Scotland, and the Prior of the Knights Templar in Scotland, who was the Preceptor of Torphichen, participated, by virtue of that office, in the Scottish government until the Protestant Reformation in Scotland. Therefore, in Scotland, there was no need for the Templars to transform themselves into anything else. Secondly, the mysterious Mount Heredom never existed. The term "Heredom" was merely a popular name in many degrees fabricated in Europe in the eighteenth century, and, according to Mackey's *Encyclopedia of Freemasonry*, the word "Heredom" derives from the Greek words "Hierōs," meaning "holy," and "Dōmos," meaning "house," so that the term "Heredom" signifies the Holy House of Masonry. Thirdly, the Templars never had any "secrets" so important that would endanger one's life by simply keeping them.

It is worth pointing out that one of the most important and oldest mottos of the 30th degree of the A.A.S.R. is: "Nec proditor Nec proditus innocens foret," which means that neither the betrayer nor the betrayed can be innocent. The Order of the Knights Templar was betrayed by some of its own knights as well as by its secular head, namely, King Philip IV of France, and by its ecclesiastical head, namely, Pope Clement V. However, the Order of the Knights Templar itself had betrayed the ancient pure Christian ethos, which the Templars were supposed to safeguard. In fact, the Knights Templar gave in to the temptations of bloody religious wars and avarice. Not only did the Templars conduct a ruthless religious war and loot several areas in Byzantium and the Middle East, but they also accumulated huge financial wealth by trading money. The Order of the Knights Templar created an international banking network, became a banker of monarchs for their mortgages, and was offering loans to finance wars through the Order's Paris headquarters.

Leaving aside every non-Masonic neo-Templar organization, which may pursue its own peculiar agenda, I should stress that those who can understand the esoteric teachings of Freemasonry are aware that the 30th degree of the A.A.S.R. uses the history of the Knights Templar neither in order to teach the "merits" of usury and "holy wars" nor in order to "sell" defunct chivalric titles, but in order to urge Freemasons to contemplate moral values and human rights and in order to transform Freemasons into Crusaders of Humanism.

Intimately related to the 30th degree is the ancient Egyptian legend of Osiris, in the sense that, from the perspective of a Knight Kadosh, the legend of Osiris symbolizes, firstly, the destruction of the Order as a result of the slain of Hiram Abiff, a martyr of fidelity to a sacred obligation, and, secondly, the Freemasons' attempt to raise Hiram Abiff as "the radical intelligence," what the Kabbalists call Geburah, which symbolically corresponds to Horus, or "Horus Abiff."

The 31st and the 32nd degrees constitute the Consistory, and they are both worked in full. The 31st degree of the Ancient and Accepted Scottish Rite is called Grand Inspector Inquisitor Commander. This degree is conferred in a Supreme Tribunal wherein the candidate is charged to oversee the observation of Freemasonic justice. A 31st degree Mason is introduced to representatives of great law givers of the past, such as Moses, Zoroaster, Socrates, Confucius, Alfred the Great King of Saxon England, etc., and is counseled to focus one's mind on the real Christian justice, which has been clarified by Jesus Christ as follows: "if you forgive others their trespasses, your heavenly Father will also forgive you. But if you do not forgive others their trespasses, neither will your Father forgive your trespasses . . . For with what judgment you judge, you shall be judged: and with what measure you mete, it shall be measured to you" (Matthew 6:14-15, 7:2). "Judge not according to the appearance, but judge righteous judgment" (John 7:24). "Blessed are the merciful: for they shall obtain mercy" (Matthew 5:7).

In the 31st degree, Scottish Rite Masons are taught that Justice and Equity are the watchwords of the Order, and that their duty is to administer the justice of equity, of right judgment, and of mercy. The term "Inquisitor" means one who seeks, searches for, and investigates the truth. The Sacred Words of the 31st degree are given as follows: one says "Tsedakah," meaning justice, the other replies by saying "Mishor," meaning equity, and then they both say "Amen."

In addition to the duties of a judge, the members of the 31st degree have to perform the following duties: to inquire into and scrutinize the work of subordinate Masonic Bodies; to safeguard that the recipients of the higher administrative degrees are not unnecessarily multiplied and that improper persons are carefully excluded from membership; and to see that, in their life and conversation, Freemasons bear testimony to the excellence of the Order's ethos.

The 32nd degree of the Ancient and Accepted Scottish Rite is called Sublime Prince of the Royal Secret and counsels charity and tolerance towards all humankind. This is exemplified by a symbolic pilgrimage in search of truth, when the candidate is conducted around the "Camp of Chivalry" where the respective points mark Confucius, Zoroaster, Buddha, Moses, Hermes Trismegistus, Plato, Jesus of Nazareth, and Muhammad. Here, within the Consistory, the candidate is able to realize and appreciate the moral content of the renowned religions and philosophies of the world. Finally, during one's initiation into the 32nd degree of the Ancient and Accepted Scottish Rite, the aspirant is taught that the pillars of the symbolic Temple that Freemasons try to erect are Freedom, Justice, Reason, and Love. In other words, the members of the 32nd degree realize that, when traditional Masonic rituals refer to the rebuilding of King Solomon's Temple, they do not refer to a literal, material project but to a Biblical symbol of a spiritual world order. This is the essence of the "Royal Secret," which is communicated to the candidate in the 32nd degree. Therefore, it is a huge mistake to confuse the Masonic vision of rebuilding a *symbolic* Jerusalem Temple (which symbolizes a new humanity) with any vision of actually building a *material, stone* Jerusalem Temple. In the hands of a Sublime Prince of the Royal Secret, a Crusader's sword becomes a symbol of the sword of Reason and of the divine Spirit, and a Sublime Prince of the Royal Secret uses this spiritual sword in order to repel falsehood and dishonor in whatever guise they may appear. In view of the foregoing, the attempt of the Modern and Perfecting Rite of Symbolic Masonry to dereligionize Freemasonry and spiritualize religion is in consonance with the inner humanistic ethos of the 32nd degree of the A.A.S.R.

The Sacred Words of the 32nd degree are given as follows: one says "SALIX," the other replies by saying "NONI(S)," and then they both say "TENGU." The words "SALIX NONI(S) TENGU" are scrambled and constitute a Masonic cipher that can be interpreted as follows: "LUX IN-EN(S) AGIT NOS," which is a Latin expression meaning "THE LIGHT THAT IS IN US GUIDES US."

The active members of the 33rd degree constitute the Supreme Council. Based on the inner humanistic ethos of the 32nd degree, which I have just delineated, the members of the 33rd degree undertake the duties of encouraging charity and fraternal love throughout the Order and preserving the ethos and the statutes of the Rite. Thus, the motto of the 33rd degree is "Deus Meumque Jus," meaning "God and My Right." Furthermore, according to the 33rd-degree Obligation that was instituted in the nineteenth century by the Southern Jurisdiction of the A.A.S.R. for the U.S.A., the members of the 33rd degree should cultivate humanism and a humanistic approach to religion, and they make the following declaration: "it is Virtue alone that can make us respectable, and religion that blesses us with happiness." The Sacred Word of the 33rd degree is the following: "Mi kamocha Ba'elim Adonai?," meaning "Who is like you in strength, O Lord?" (Exodus 15:11). Hence, whereas the Sacred Words of the 32nd degree imply that we, as humans and senior initiates, are partakers of the deity and carriers of an inner light, which underpins our progress in the deity, the Sacred Word of the 33rd degree implies that the whole fullness of the absolute Being transcends us.

The members of the 33rd degree realize and are explicitly taught that their object is not to rebuild the material Temple of King Solomon, but a moral temple, wherein truth and love will dwell, and wherein people will live as an ecumenical brotherhood abiding by the laws of eternal equity and justice. Moreover, the members of the 33rd degree realize and are explicitly taught that they have not to avenge the murder of Hiram Abiff, who is a symbol of Masonic wisdom, which ignorance, lust for power, and falsehood have concealed from many people, but they must go on, in search of the laws that regulate the moral world.

The human being is both good and bad, in the sense that, at times, good prevails over evil, and, at others, evil prevails over good. Human nature is characterized by the dualistic expressions of good and evil, just and unjust, true and false, beautiful and ugly. In order to bridge the abyss of dualism, humans invented religion. In particular, humans, once they become conscious of their own suffering, turn to a merciful divine being and ask for divine intervention to help them resolve their problems. The humanistic approach to religion that is promoted by the 33rd degree of the A.A.S.R. comprises the following principles: (1) religion is an invention of thinking humanity; (2) religion is meaningful only if and to the extent that it helps humans to resolve their existential problems; (3) religion and science are expressions of human creativity and mechanisms of adaptation of the human species, and, therefore, religion and science must be reconciled; (4) the cultivation of moral consciousness, through both religious and non-religious anthropologies, leads the most developed minds to the conclusion that, even though humanity may not be ready to unite in one religious formula, it can unite morally within the framework of certain universal moral norms, to which all religions conform.

V.M: Given that one of the declared goals and structural characteristics of the Modern and Perfecting Rite of Symbolic Masonry is the dereligionization of Freemasonry, the Modern and Perfecting Rite of Symbolic Masonry dismisses any religious or quasi-religious aspect or practice of the traditional rituals of the English Symbolic Masonry and the Scottish Rite, but, in principle, it endorses the humanistic approach to religion that is promoted by the 33rd degree of the A.A.S.R., because the latter's attempt to refine and, indeed, spiritualize religion and to promote a type of moral ecumenism, is in consonance with the type of spirituality that is promoted by the Modern and Perfecting Rite of Symbolic Masonry. However, the Modern and Perfecting Rite of Symbolic Masonry explicitly maintains that its project for the spiritualization of religion consists in substituting the traditional "gods" of religions with the ideal of the man-god, which is focused on the idea of wisdom. Thus, the "man-god" of the Modern and Perfecting Rite of Symbolic Masonry is a perfectly wise human being, and the project of the Modern and Perfecting Rite of Symbolic Masonry for the spiritualization of religion implies that wisdom, instead of traditional practices of worship, should be the primary value towards which humans should aspire.

As regards the history and the dynamics of the "higher degrees," that is, the ultra-Craft degrees, we must not lose sight of the fact that, just as the British establishment has used the British model of Symbolic Masonry as a tool for cultural diplomacy, so the American establishment and the French establishment have used Masonic Orders of the "higher degrees," such as the Scottish Rite and Masonic Templar Orders, as American and French tools for cultural diplomacy, respectively. In general, the history of Freemasonry is intertwined with geopolitics and international affairs. Additionally, the history of Freemasonry presents numerous cases in which members of the social establishment join Freemasonry in order to manipulate it from the inside and profane its spiritual and political core.

Far from permitting an institution as powerful as Freemasonry to operate and develop freely and peacefully, many members of the ruling elites have been actively involved in the formation and management of Freemasonic institutions for the sake of the social establishment and in order to serve the vested interests of these particular elites. Thus, in the nineteenth and the twentieth centuries, the profane world influenced Freemasonry more than Freemasonry influenced the profane world. Revolting against this deep corruption that Freemasonry has suffered in its original truth, the Autonomous Order of the Modern and Perfecting Rite of Symbolic Masonry emerged at the dawn of the twenty-first century as the bearer of a Freemasonic Reformation and a New Enlightenment.

The Autonomous Order of the Modern and Perfecting Rite of Symbolic Masonry creates only Symbolic Masons, and it does not recognize any Masonic degree as superior to the Master Mason degree. However, the Autonomous Order of the Modern and Perfecting Rite of Symbolic Masonry has incorporated in its three degrees many significant elements and teachings of several Masonic systems of "higher degrees," such as the Ancient and Accepted Scottish Rite. Indeed, every major philosophical and political teaching of the 33 degrees of the Ancient and Accepted Scottish Rite is included in the 3 degrees of the Modern and Perfecting Rite of Symbolic Masonry, and we have already presented to you the standard teachings and symbols of each and every one of the degrees of the A.A.S.R. Indeed, the Modern and Perfecting Rite of Symbolic Masonry is a universal system of Symbolic Masonry that has absorbed several ultra-Craft Rites and degrees, and its material is cast in such a manner as to provide a synthetic understanding of every significant aspect of the entire history of Freemasonry, create erudite cultural builders, serve an esoteric philosophical vision of universal unity, and operate as a consistent system of Symbolic Masonry and rigorous scholarship, without needing a mosaic of additional Masonic degrees, ceremonies, and Orders.

The Autonomous Order of the Modern and Perfecting Rite of Symbolic Masonry relieves our fellow humans from an unnecessary and confusing segmentation of Freemasonry into many different ultra-Craft degrees and Orders. Thus, the Autonomous Order of the Modern and Perfecting Rite of Symbolic Masonry brings the most important elements of Symbolic Masonry, Royal Arch Masonry, Scottish Rite Masonry, and Egyptian Rite Masonry into one "house." It would not, therefore, be an exaggeration to maintain that a Master Mason of the Modern and Perfecting Rite of Symbolic Masonry is actually a true expert in the entire spectrum of Masonry, including both Craft and ultra-Craft Rites.

The major goal of the Autonomous Order of the Modern and Perfecting Rite of Symbolic Masonry is to preserve, protect, defend, teach, and propagate the Modern and Perfecting Rite of Symbolic Masonry internationally. The Modern and Perfecting Rite of Symbolic Masonry signifies a substantive reform of Symbolic Masonry on the basis of the following principles:

Firstly, the Modern and Perfecting Rite of Symbolic Masonry has shifted the center of gravity of Symbolic Masonry from mythology, religious texts, didactic tales, and complex rituality to philosophy, science, and psychoanalysis. For this reason, the Modern and Perfecting Rite of Symbolic Masonry is based on Operative Masonry as a source of inspiration, but it dismisses the use of religious Masonic rituals, and its ceremonies are carried out according to Masonic dramas and catechisms based on philosophy, science, and psychoanalysis. Therefore, the Autonomous Order of the Modern and Perfecting Rite of Symbolic Masonry understands and practices Freemasonry in a way that is significantly different from the way in which the Grand Lodges of the British Isles formed Symbolic Masonry in the eighteenth and the nineteenth centuries.

Secondly, the Modern and Perfecting Rite of Symbolic Masonry is a genuinely universal Freemasonic Rite, and, for this reason, it is not restricted territorially to the level of national institutions, but it perceives and treats the entire world as a unified Freemasonic Jurisdiction, and it maintains the right to found Lodges and Regional Directorates of this Rite internationally. The supreme, overarching, and sovereign governing body of every Lodge and every Regional Directorate of the Modern and Perfecting Rite of Symbolic Masonry is the Grand Lodge of the Autonomous Order of the Modern and Perfecting Rite of Symbolic Masonry. Additionally, in accordance with its principle of universality, the Autonomous Order of the Modern and Perfecting Rite of Symbolic Masonry admits both men and women to membership, does not require Freemasons to declare a religious faith, and has eliminated every religious or quasi-religious practice from its ceremonies.

Thirdly, the Modern and Perfecting Rite of Symbolic Masonry is humanistic, and it endorses and promotes scholarly rigor. Its interests extend across all scholarly disciplines, namely, across the humanities, the social sciences, and the natural sciences. It is within this context that the Autonomous Order of the Modern and Perfecting Rite of Symbolic Masonry permits and encourages political and religious discussion within its Lodges. Our Order seeks to create fulfilled human beings. The great

Prussian philosopher, linguist, educationalist, and diplomat Wilhelm von Humboldt has pointedly argued that the core principle and requirement of a fulfilled human being is the ability to inquire and create in a free and rational way. Thus, Humboldt promoted the concept of "holistic" academic education (in German, "Bildung"), he identified knowledge with power, and he identified education with liberty.

According to the Modern and Perfecting Rite of Symbolic Masonry, the chief objects as a Master Mason are to reform consciousness and restructure reality along the lines of this Order.

The Modern and Perfecting Rite of Symbolic Masonry is building a republic of god-kings, all equally holy, blessed, glorious, and royal. The members of the Modern and Perfecting Rite of Symbolic Masonry humanize the deity, deify humanity, and desire rational enlightenment.

The Autonomous Order of the Modern and Perfecting Rite of Symbolic Masonry promotes a model of statesmanship that is characterized by a humanistic variety of cultural aristocracy and radical visions of popular sovereignty. The origins of this model of statesmanship can be traced back to ancient Sparta's genuine Doric model of statesmanship, known as "damocracy" (Doric form of "democracy"), which was formed by the Spartan lawgiver Lycurgus (eighth century B.C.), and it was based on the following two principles: (i) *the political equality of the citizens*, namely, the members of Sparta's popular deliberative assembly, known as the "Apella" (which secured equal right of speech and equality of all the citizens before the law); (ii) *the citizen's personal value*, which was measured according to the virtue and the spirituality that one manifested through the manner in which one was relating to and utilizing the established system of political equality. Thus, from the perspective of the Doric spirituality and politology, democracy and political equality refer to the rules that regulate the relations between the members of a spiritual aristocracy founded on the principle of the "sacred" and expressing the One, the Illuminated "Archagētes" (supreme leader), and have nothing to do with materialist and culturally plebeian forms of democracy. When the spirit of Sparta's damocracy – which dictates that the citizens should be judged and evaluated according to their true value (that is, inner nobility) – was lost, the citizens' judgments and values were darkened and blurred, and the citizens started being judged and evaluated according to false values (such as material wealth, self promotion, public relations, etc.), which prevailed in the modern era (especially in the context of bourgeois democracy or liberal oligarchy). However, the aforementioned Doric political ethos was further developed and intellectually enriched by Plato's philosophy, Jesus Christ's teachings, socialist and communist schools of thought and social movements, and modern revolutionary political thought.

Brother/Sister . . . (*name and surname of the Candidate*), the motto of a true Master Mason is Freedom with order, Equality with honor for legitimate authority, and Fraternity with justice."